CW01638808

The state of the countryside 2000

Distributed by:
Countryside Agency Publications
PO Box 125
Wetherby
West Yorkshire LS23 7EP

Tel: 0870 120 6466
Fax: 0870 120 6467
Website: www.countryside.gov.uk
Minicom: 0870 120 7405 (for the hard of hearing)

Foreword

The countryside matters. It matters to those who live there. It matters to those who make their living there. It matters to those in towns who never go there. In a year that will be remembered for the passage of the Countryside and Rights of Way Bill through Parliament and the publication of a Rural White Paper, there can be no doubt that the countryside matters more and more.

As concern for, and interest in, rural England grows, so should our understanding. We need to know what really is happening in the countryside. Rhetoric and anecdotes are not enough. That is why I am proud that the Countryside Agency is publishing its second State of the Countryside Report.

It is a fascinating compendium of information about the countryside with important data about how land is used for business and for enjoyment, what it is like to live in or visit the countryside, and environmental trends. The facts speak for themselves. They show that for many who live and work in rural England life is prosperous and enjoyable. But behind the rosy image of the rural idyll lie some very real problems; problems of rural isolation, a declining environment, pressurised and declining services and a vulnerable rural economy.

The facts also identify some fears about the future. There is concern that the most valued aspects of rural life such as a strong sense of community and security are threatened. It will be sad if future reports demonstrate that these fears have become a reality.

But the State of the Countryside 2000 is more than an encyclopaedia of facts. It is a valuable tool. Equipped with well researched data, we can take informed action to reduce undesirable changes taking place in the countryside. Without good intelligence we simply grope in the dark and risk designing ill-fitting policies. The document should be used by all of us with an interest in the welfare of rural England to inform our actions and policies. This year we intend to publish a series of regional reports which we hope will be helpful to those working at that level.

We have drawn information for this report from many sources. I thank all those individuals and organisations who have contributed.

I hope all that read this document find it both informative and useful and that the facts within it can be brought to bear on the decisions of those who shape our countryside.

Ewen Cameron
Chairman

Contents

1 Introduction

Monitoring and evaluating the state of the countryside is an important part of the Countryside Agency's work. It enables others to base their work on facts. It allows a proper evaluation of past decisions and policies – whether that is the collective outcome of the decisions people take as individuals, or the outcome of policies adopted by government at the national or local level. We published our first State of the Countryside report in April 1999. This second report updates that, but also includes some important new developments. In addition, we will publish a set of accompanying regional reports during 2000.

Defining 'rural'

Most people have an image of what is meant by 'rural'. Yet, defining rural for consistent reporting is challenging. There are many administrative definitions. Some administrative units that form the basis for collecting and reporting information do not distinguish rural from urban.

For future reports, the Countryside Agency will use settlement structure, population density, land use and land cover to improve our definition of what we mean by rural at ward level. In the meantime, this report uses the definition employed by the former Rural Development Commission (RDC) which classified rural local authority districts and unitary authorities as shown on the map on Page 65[1], unless otherwise noted.

Change and loss

This report gives an overview of rural facts and trends and urban comparisons, and also explores how people view the countryside. It reveals a complex picture. People who live in the country often enjoy a better quality of life than those living in towns, yet some of the findings of the report identify serious causes for concern. Some people in the countryside may enjoy 'the good life', but others suffer exclusion and isolation. This disadvantage can be hard to uncover because it is often masked by the proximity of affluence.

England's rural communities are going through a period of great change. Some of the things people most value about life in the

1. The RDC classification was itself based on three other lists of rural districts:
– the Office of National Statistics (ONS) 'Classification of Local Authority Districts'. This used data from the 1991 Census to classify areas with similar characteristics into groups;
– the National Council of Voluntary Organizations (NCVO) list, based primarily on population density;
– the DETR list of (pre~reorganisation) districts, included within the 1995 Rural White Paper.

countryside are being eroded – and that is worrying them. There is an unsettling fear that villages and market towns are losing their sense of community, as well as the relative security and freedom from crime which many have enjoyed for a long time. The facts tend to support this, with some crimes increasing disproportionately in rural areas. Vehicle crime, for example, rose by 24% between 1991 and 1995, in rural areas, compared with 4% in urban areas and 10% in inner cities.

It is clear that some people living in the countryside enjoy prosperity. The affluent and mobile may enjoy a good quality of life, but a significant minority suffers serious disadvantage. Average weekly wages are lowest in rural counties such as Cornwall, Northumberland and Shropshire. To make matters worse, many essential rural services are either closing or face the threat of closure. This creates particular problems for the less well-off trying to get basic services if their post office, doctors' surgery or village shop has disappeared.

There are threats, too, to the health of the rural economy. On the surface, it may look vigorous, but an in-depth examination reveals a more mixed picture: sectors of that economy are vulnerable to change, and some areas of rural England have serious structural weaknesses. Many market towns which once enjoyed an important status in county life are no longer centres of commerce and industry, or the social hub for their rural hinterlands that they once were.

What is causing these changes? Partly, our rural communities are subject to wider changes including economic, social, cultural and environmental pressures that may be global in their impact. Take farming: the value of our agricultural output has collapsed in the face of low world commodity prices and the high value of sterling. Coupled with other changes in English agriculture, this is putting enormous pressure on farming communities, and their livelihoods and well-being, as well as on the environment, which has seen, for example, a rapid decline in once-common farmland birds.

Social exclusion is a further problem. It is increasingly difficult for young people and those on lower incomes to continue to live in rural areas, in the face of increased demand for houses and rising prices. This is made worse by fewer affordable houses being built there.

On the roads, more and more vehicles are making life hazardous for pedestrians and cyclists, as well as for motorists themselves. Traffic is rising faster on rural roads than on others. This damages the quality of life in other ways, too. Parents may worry that it is unsafe for them to let their children out to play – a common enough concern in towns that is now being echoed in some rural areas.

Signs of hope

Yet there are signs of hope. Research shows that rural communities have kept a stronger sense of identity and unity than many urban counterparts. Incomers may be responsible for bringing about change on the rural scene, but many also make an important contribution to their communities. In addition, country dwellers are generally healthier than their urban counterparts, even if they may face greater difficulty in getting access to health care.

Millions continue to enjoy visiting or holidaying in the countryside, and tourism and recreation bring jobs and contribute in a big way to rural economies. There is also evidence that rural dwellers are increasingly finding work in the growth sectors of the economy, such as finance and services. Information and communication technology is helping to create new opportunities for rural-based businesses.

Many people believe the countryside offers a good place to live and would move there if they could. Attitude surveys also reveal strong public concern for the countryside, with more people recognising its value. This is shown, for example, by growing membership of organisations such as the National Trust and the RSPB, as well as wide political commitment to 'sustainable development'. In addition, environmental land management is helping create appreciable numbers of jobs.

Farmers are experiencing difficult times, yet people are recognising the important role they play in producing food and managing the countryside. Innovation and increased funding are helping farmers to add value to their produce or diversify their businesses and are beginning to offer at least some new ways forward as an aid to industry restructuring.

And there are some common themes emerging that offer a new future for rural communities and economies. These include stronger partnership-based working and greater local consultation, and an increasing desire for communities to solve their own problems. This has already been seen in the enormous success of our Millennium Greens and the Village Design initiatives.

And in more detail...

This second State of the Countryside Report paints a broad picture of rural England. Some more detailed analyses can be found in the sources referenced, but we acknowledge some gaps, and, wherever possible, we plan to find ways to ensure that these are filled for future reports. Part of this work involves preparing a set of rural 'indicators' which will complement the DETR 'indicators of sustainable development' (DETR, 1999a).

2 Diverse character and outstanding beauty

Andy Tryner/Countryside Agency

Knipton, Leicestershire.

The English countryside is distinctive for its diverse landscapes and cultural heritage – the outcome of a synergy between nature and people. This makes for a dynamic and evolving countryside. But human activity has also had a considerable negative impact on the landscapes and natural resources of the English countryside.

There is appreciable soil erosion, particularly from arable land. While the chemical quality of England's waterways is improving, important aspects of their physical condition have, in many cases, declined. Biodiversity, especially as indicated by wild bird populations, has decreased in many parts of the countryside. Valued monuments are at risk from damage or destruction.

There is also a high level of public concern for the countryside, and growing interest, in many rural areas, in maintaining cultural traditions, as well as developing new ones. Sites of Special Scientific Interest and Biodiversity Action Plans, for example, seek to address the loss of biodiversity; National Parks and Areas of Outstanding Natural Beauty recognise high-value landscapes of national importance; while Community Forests aim to regenerate attractive and accessible countryside around towns.

Countryside character

The diverse character of the English countryside is partly reflected in the main categories of land cover (Figure 2.1). While managed grassland and arable land account for the largest area, there are appreciable areas of semi-natural vegetation and forestry and woodland.

Figure 2.1 Land cover in England, 1990

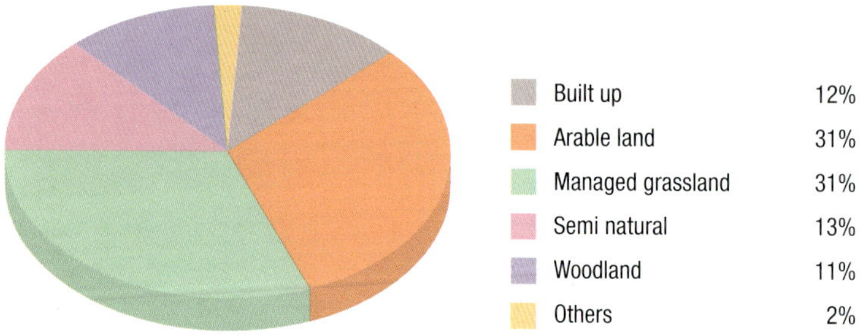

Source: Barr et al (1993)

Designation of National Parks, Areas of Outstanding Natural Beauty and Heritage Coasts recognises the special character and high landscape value of particular areas. Together these account for nearly one quarter of England's land area (see map on Page 68).

- There are eight National Parks, covering a total of 9,934 km^2 (7.6% of England's land area)[2].
- Thirty-seven Areas of Outstanding Natural Beauty cover a further 20,393 km^2 (15.6% of England's land area).
- Heritage Coasts extend to total of 1,027 km length – 35% of England's coastline.

The full diversity of the character of the English countryside is vividly portrayed by the Countryside Agency's 159 'countryside character areas'. These have been identified, mapped and described on the basis of both physical and cultural/historical variables, namely

2. In addition, the Countryside Agency has begun the process of designating the New Forest as a National Park, and expects to make the Designation Order by Autumn 2001 and invite the Secretary of State to confirm it. The Agency is also considering whether there should be a National Park in the South Downs.

altitude, landform, ecological characteristics, land capability, surface geology, farm types, settlement patterns, woodland cover, field density and pattern, visible archaeology, industrial history and designed parkland. The character areas and their descriptions aim to inform decision making and shape change, nationally and regionally, so as to maintain and enhance local distinctiveness (Countryside Agency, 1999a). The 159 areas are shown on the map on Page 66.[3]

Soils

Soils take between 1,000–10,000 years to form (Edwards & Withers, 1998) and erode naturally under the action of water and wind. Most types of farming accelerate soil erosion to some degree. Soils are at greatest risk under continuous intensive cropping and least at risk under permanent vegetation.

- This is shown by comparing soil erosion risk (Figure 2.2) with agricultural land use (Figure 2.3).
- It is also illustrated by recent research which estimated that about 2.2 million tonnes of soil per year are lost from a total of 26,300 km^2 of arable land in England through erosion by water. Erosion is not only from steeply sloping land: some 13% of the total loss from heavy arable soils is from flat to moderately sloping land[4] (SSLRC, 2000).

Water

The chemical water quality of England's rivers is improving. Comparison of three-year rolling averages indicates an overall net improvement in chemical water quality across all regions of around 24%[5] between 1988–90 and 1996–98, with every region showing a positive net increase (Environment Agency, personal communication, 1999).

In contrast, **the physical condition of some of England's waterways is declining,** at least in some aspects.

- Surveys of rivers and streams in England and Wales in 1994–97 found that there were few remaining 'pristine' lowland channels flowing through semi-natural landscapes. Some 13.6% of sites in England and Wales had severely modified channels. Land drainage, flood defence, intensive agriculture and urban development have all resulted in extensive reinforcement and re-sectioning of river banks and channel impoundment, with a significant reduction in habitat diversity along stretches of some rivers (Environment Agency & SEPA, 1998).
- Areas near a number of rivers are increasingly vulnerable to colonisation by invasive alien plant species, indicated by the widespread occurrence of Giant Hogweed, Japanese Knotweed and Himalayan Balsam. In places, these species have significantly

3. National character areas are being further analysed in detail for counties and districts. This systematic, descriptive information helps to direct the management of change at a local level and helps people to have a better understanding of the context of their local environment and 'sense of place'. The active application of landscape character assessment, both as Supplemenay Planning Guidance and as the basis for structure and local plan polices helps to guide the quality of development in the countryside.

4. These estimates do not include soil lost through wind erosion, which particularly affects lighter textured soils.

5. As indicated by measurements of Biochemical Oxygen Demand, ammonia and dissolved carbon dioxide at sample sites.

Figure 2.2 Estimated vulnerability to erosion of soils in England (derived from a statistical analysis of measurements taken at National Soil Inventory Nodes)

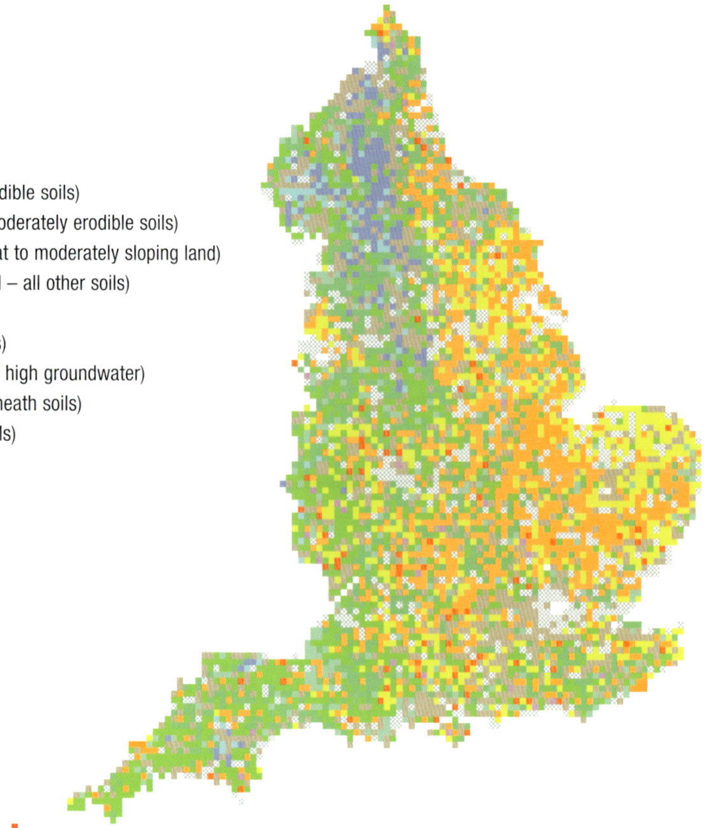

- Land class 1 — Arable (steep land with highly erodible soils)
- Land class 2 — Arable (slightly steep land with moderately erodible soils)
- Land class 3 — Arable (heavy-textured soils on flat to moderately sloping land)
- Land class 4 — Arable (flat to slightly sloping land – all other soils)
- Land class 5 — Grassland (freely draining soils)
- Land class 6 — Grassland (slowly permeable soils)
- Land class 7 — Grassland (waterlogged soils with high groundwater)
- Land class 8 — Upland grazing (dry moorland or heath soils)
- Land class 9 — Upland grazing (wet moorland soils)
- Land class 10 — Others

Source: Derived from data provided by Soil Survey and Land Research Centre

Figure 2.3 Dominant farm type by parish, England, 1998 (calculated using number of holdings)

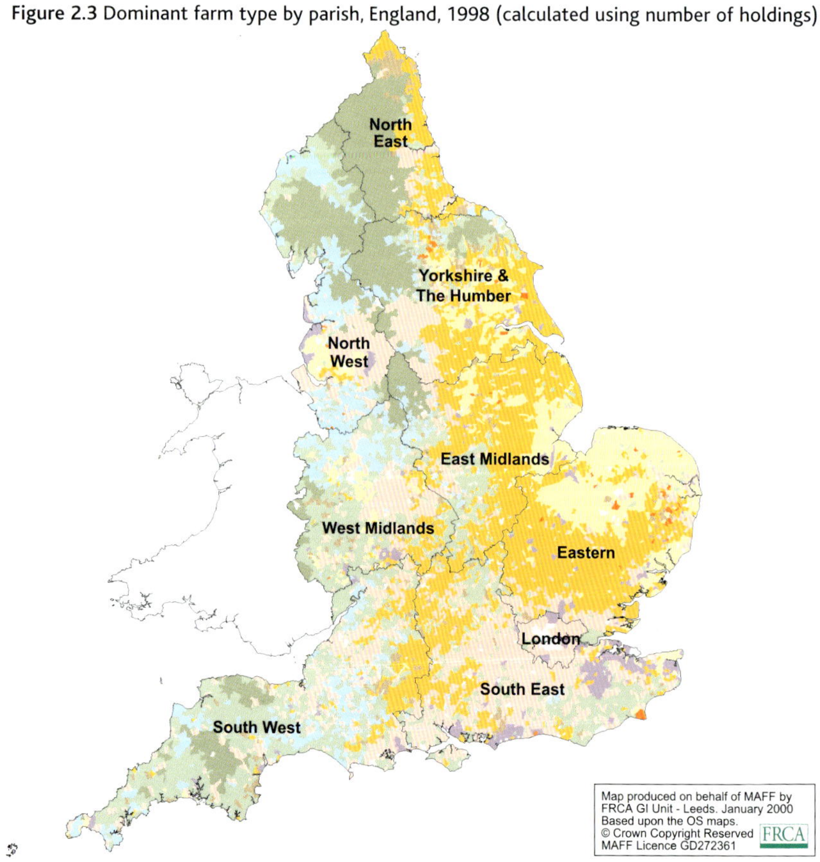

- Cereals
- Mixed
- Horticulture
- Dairy
- Pigs and poultry
- Cattle and sheep (LFA)
- Cattle and sheep (lowland)
- General cropping
- Other type
- No data available
- Government Office boundary

Data source: Agricultural Census 1998 (MAFF)

impacted on native flora and fauna (Cronk & Fuller, 1995; Environment Agency, 1996).

Air

Despite the association of the countryside with fresh air and the perception that the countryside is less polluted than towns[6], rural areas sometimes experience levels of air pollution greater than those in urban areas (Environment Agency, 2000).

- Monitoring sites in rural areas record, in general, higher concentrations of ground-level ozone than sites in urban areas, and fail government human health standards of 50 ppb (100g/m^3), on average one day in 12.
- Ground-level ozone concentrations above limits critical for natural vegetation and arable crops are commonly experienced throughout England, particularly in the south. There has been no clear trend over the past decade, but the problem seems likely to persist.
- Despite substantial reductions in sulphur emissions in recent years, critical loads for acidification will still be exceeded in Cumbria and across the Pennines in 2010. The pattern of ecological recovery is uncertain.
- Deposition of nutrient nitrogen at levels above those critical for characteristic heathland plant communities is widespread in upland areas. The ability of damaged ecosystems to recover is unknown, but is likely to take decades.

Biodiversity

The number and extent of areas designated in order to protect high quality habitats and particular species has increased appreciably in recent years (eg. see Figures 2.6 and 2.7). However, **biodiversity in the countryside continues to decline steeply** (eg. see Figure 2.8).

Special areas designated to protect habitats and wildlife cover some 19,678 km^2 (14.9 % of England's land area). On 31 March 1999 there were (English Nature, 1999):

- 4,039 Sites of Special Scientific Interest covering a total of 1,035,609 ha (7.84% of England) (see Figures 2.4 and 2.5);
- 197 National Nature Reserves covering a total of 79,526 ha (0.60% of England) (see Figure 2.6);
- 612 Local Nature Reserves, covering over 29,245 ha (0.22% of England) (see Figure 2.7);
- 72 Ramsar Sites[7] covering a total of 368,750 ha (2.80% of England);
- 76 Special Protection Areas[8] covering a total of 454,713 ha (3.44% of England).

In addition, in accordance with the 92/43/EEC Directive on the Conservation of Natural Habitats, Wild Fauna and Flora, by March 1999 the DETR had submitted a list of 147 candidate Special Areas of

6. See Page 15.

7. Ramsar sites are areas which have been formally listed as Wetlands of International Importance by the Secretary of State in accordance with the Ramsar Convention (1973).

8. Special Protection Areas (SPAs) are designated by the Secretary of State under Directive 79/409/EEC on the Conservation of Wild Birds. Many areas qualify for both SPA and Ramsar designations.

Figure 2.4 Sites of Special Scientific Interest (SSSIs) and Natural Areas in England, 1999

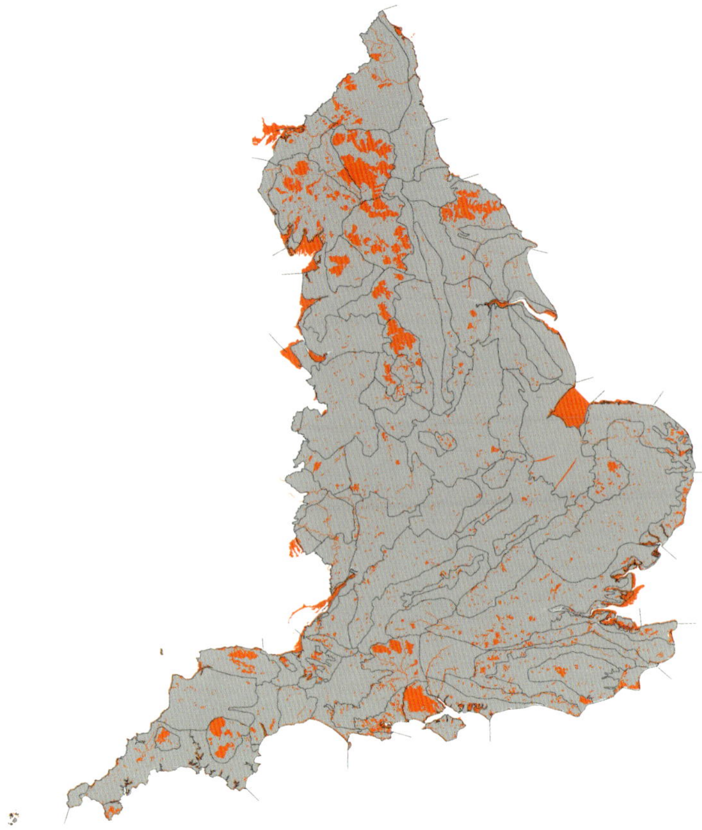

Source: FRCA, MAFF (personal communication, 1999) and English Nature (personal communication, 1999)

Conservation (SACs) (representing a total area of 611,711 ha, some 4.64% of England) to the European Commission.

Biodiversity in the wider countryside is being addressed through the development of Biodiversity Action Plans, within a framework of Natural Areas (see Figure 2.4) (English Nature, Countryside Commission, 1996). In the farming context, schemes that should contribute to maintaining or improving biodiversity include Countryside Stewardship, Environmentally Sensitive Areas and the Organic Aid Scheme.

Figure 2.5 Overall condition of SSSI features

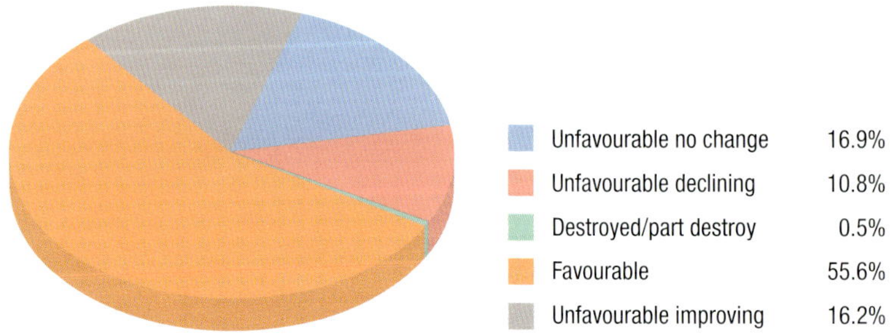

Source: English Nature (1999)

Figure 2.6 Number and area of National Nature Reserves in England, 1991–1999

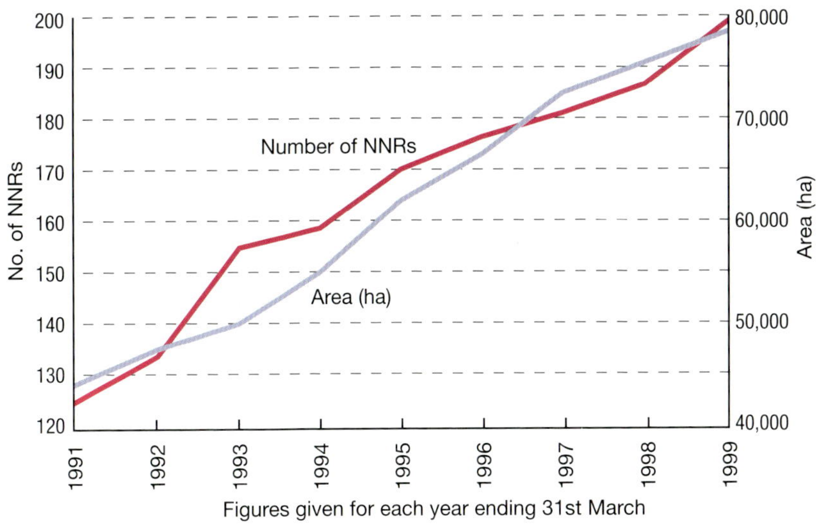

Source: English Nature (1999)

Figure 2.7 Number and area of Local Nature Reserves in England, 1991–1999

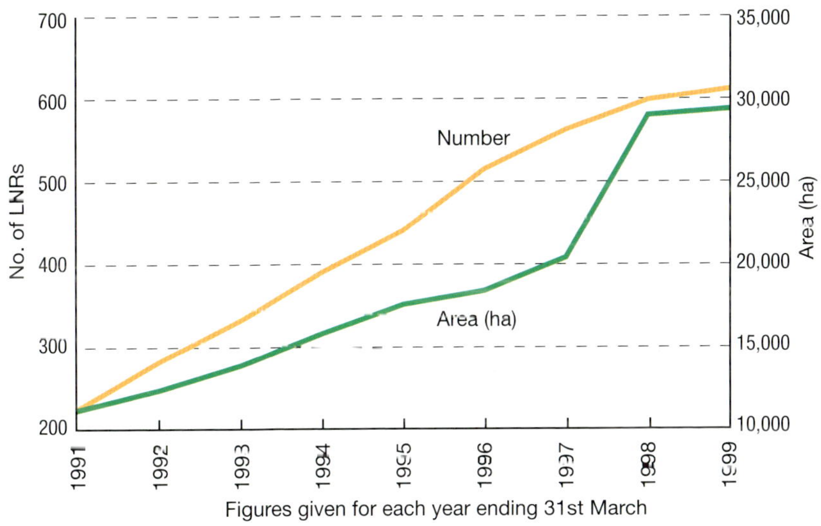

Source: English Nature (1999)

Currently, the most useful indicator of biodiversity in the wider countryside is wild bird populations (DETR, 1999a). The trend (Figure 2.8) is one of **continuing and serious decline in the populations of a range of wild bird species.** This is indicative of a broader decline in habitat quality and species richness of wide areas of countryside across England (DETR, 1999a).

Agriculture continues to be the main cause of ecological damage to Sites of Special Scientific Interest, and, almost certainly, to biodiversity in the wider countryside, although new development and transport infrastructure also have an impact (English Nature, 1999).

Figure 2.8 Populations of wild birds, 1970–1998

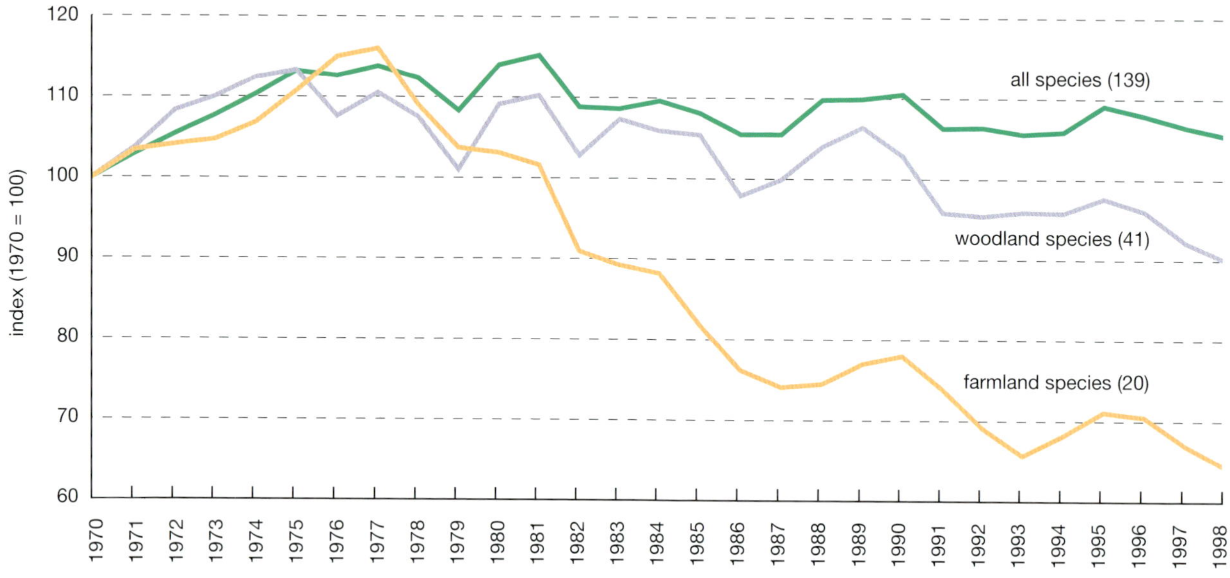

Source: DETR (1999a)

Cultural heritage

Many traditions maintain ties between people and place including customs, dialects, local design and the building materials of everyday places. The value people place on their locality and its customs is demonstrated, for example, by the growth of interest in Village Design Statements[9], Parish Maps[10], the Local Heritage Initiative, and events such as Apple Days[11] and Tree Dressing Days[12].

According to the Monuments at Risk Survey[13] (Darvill & Fulton, 1998), **many historical monuments in the countryside are at risk of damage or destruction**.

- Of a total of 1 million recorded monuments[14], some 2% are at high risk from serious damage or destruction over the next few years, and a further 28% are at medium risk of such damage and require careful monitoring.
- 30% of monuments are under threat from agriculture, the majority (27%) from arable cultivation, one of the activities most destructive of certain categories of monument and least controlled by current protective measures or legislation (forestry is also a continuing threat to monuments and their settings) (see Figure 2.9).
- Linear monuments have least incidence of high risk (1%) whilst field systems and standing buildings have the highest (2.4% and 2.7% respectively) (see Figure 2.10). Field systems are at most risk from arable management regimes, but at lowest risk (29%) where pasture and semi-natural land use predominates.

9. See Page 25.

10. See Page 25.

11. There were 600 recorded Apple Day events on 21 October 1999. Whole communities were involved, including local shops, restaurants, schools and libraries with new community orchards being planted and local varieties of fruit being rediscovered.

12. Eg. many thousands of Tree Dressing Day events took place across the country at the end of National Tree week in December 1999.

13. The Monuments at Risk Survey (MARS) provides a baseline picture of the condition of England's archaeological resource, the threats to it, and benchmarks against which future changes can be monitored.

14. As entered in the 'National Sites and Monuments Record' at January 2000.

Figure 2.9 Level of risk to monuments by land use

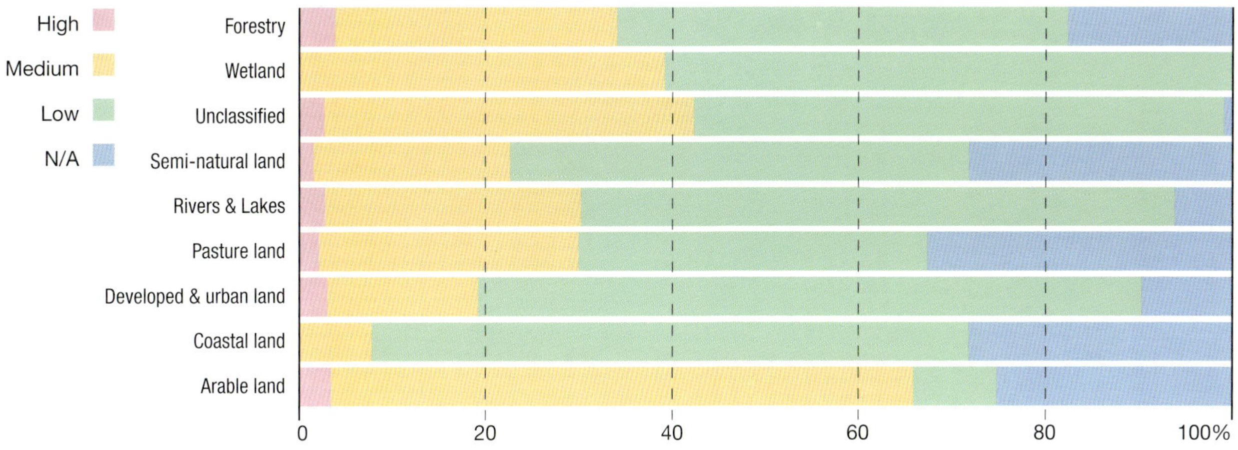

Source: Darvill & Fulton (1998)

Figure 2.10 Level of risk to monuments by monument type

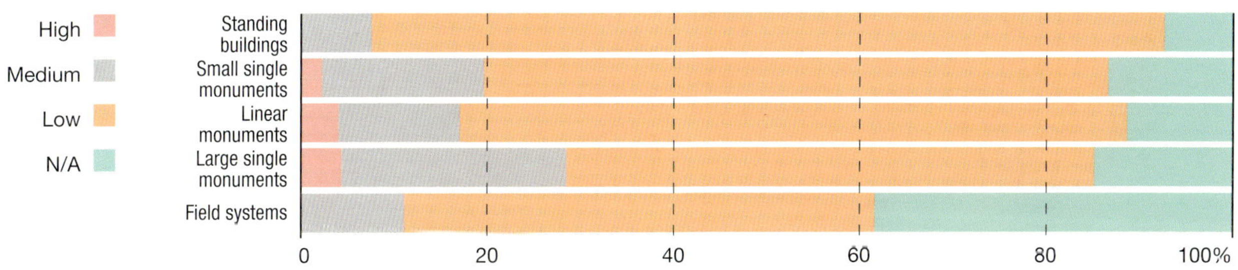

Source: Darvill & Fulton (1998)

Public perception of the countryside

Many more people would like to live in the countryside than do so at present. For example, of those questioned in the 1999 British Social Attitudes Survey[15], while only 18% said they lived in a rural location, nearly 50% said they would like to live in the countryside. Environmental benefits feature highly among the reasons for regarding the countryside as offering a better place to live: 90% of those questioned believed the countryside provided a 'healthier environment to live in'.

Social attitudes surveys also reveal a high level of public concern for the countryside. Of the people questioned in the 1999 British Social Attitudes Survey:

- 84% expressed concern 'about things that may happen to the countryside';
- 75% considered 'the countryside should be protected from development, even if this sometimes leads to fewer jobs', 80% agreed that 'it is more important to keep green-belt areas than to build new homes there', and 73% agreed that 'new housing should be built in cities, towns and villages rather than in the countryside';

15. Conducted by the National Centre for Social Research.

- 88% considered that 'industry should be prevented from causing damage to the countryside, even if this sometimes leads to higher prices';
- 69% felt that 'modern methods of farming have caused damage to the countryside', 56% agreed that 'Government should withhold some subsidies from farmers and use them to protect the countryside, even if this leads to higher prices', and 66% disagreed that 'if farmers have to choose between, producing more food and looking after the countryside, they should produce more food. However, 77% felt that 'all things considered, farmers do a good job in looking after the countryside'.

Public interest in the countryside is reflected in the considerable growth in membership of environmental organisations (Figure 2.11).

Figure 2.11 Membership (thousands) of selected environmental and countryside organisations, UK

	1971	1981	1991	1997
National Trust[16]	278	1,046	2,152	2,489
Royal Society for the Protection of Birds	98	441	852	1,007
Wildlife Trusts	64	142	233	310
World Wide Fund for Nature	12	60	227	241
Greenpeace		30	312	215
Woodland Trust		20	150	195
Ramblers Association	22	37	87	123
Friends of the Earth[17]	1	18	111	114
Council for the Protection of Rural England	21	29	45	45

Source: ONS (1999a)

However, an analysis of the 1998 British Social Attitudes Survey concluded that high levels of public concern about the environment co-exist with a deep-seated reluctance to support measures to reduce the impact of our own lifestyles on environmental quality (Christie & Jarvis, 1999).

Community Forests

Many areas of countryside around towns suffer from dereliction and development pressures; concerted efforts are needed to manage these rapidly changing landscapes. Only 7% of England is wooded, the second lowest percentage of tree cover in the European Union. In response, in 1995, the Countryside Commission initiated 12 Community Forests in England. Up to 30% of the area of each will be planted with trees to create well-wooded landscapes for nature conservation and recreational use. The Forests meet a national need for community based programmes

16. Data are for England, Wales and Northern Ireland only

17. Data are for England, Wales and Northern Ireland only

to regenerate the countryside around towns (Countryside Agency, 1999b).

- Some 26 million people (50% of England's population) live in, or within easy reach of, a Community Forest (see Figure 2.12).
- Already, over 1,033 hectares of derelict, urban-fringe land have been reclaimed for Community Forest related uses, including community activities, new cycleways and new woodland enterprise, all based on sustainable development principles.
- To date, over 8,796 hectares of existing woodland have been brought under better management, whilst 6,220 hectares of new woodland have been planted.
- Over 5,689 hectares of associated, non-woodland habitat have been created and/or brought under better management and over 783 kilometres of new hedgerows have been planted.

Figure 2.12 Areas and associated populations of Community Forests[18]

Name	Area (ha)	Population within 20km (millions)
Forest of Avon	57,300	1.0
Forest of Mercia	21,000	4.0
The Great North Forest	16,000	1.0
Great Western Community Forest	39,000	1.0
The Greenwood Community Forest	41,400	1.0
Marston Vale Community Forest	15,800	0.5
The Mersey Forest	92,500	5.0
Red Rose	76,000	4.0
South Yorkshire Forest	39,499	1.9
The Tees Forest	25,500	1.0
Thames Chase Community Forest	9,850	3.0
Watling Chase	16,250	3.0
TOTAL	450,009	26.4

Source: (Countryside Agency, 1999b)

18. See also map on Page 68.

3 Prosperous and inclusive communities

Steve Tanner/Countryside Agency

St. Neot, Cornwall.

The English countryside is distinctive not only for its landscapes, but also for its communities. The rural population has increased in recent years, and many more people would like to live in the countryside if they could. Community spirit in rural areas is rated highly, and not only by rural people; there is less crime and people are, on average, slightly healthier than their urban counterparts. Rural people participate in many social activities, and, increasingly, in various kinds of 'local action' and 'self-help' networks. Houses in rural areas are, generally, in better condition than in urban areas.

However, rural communities are changing. In many areas, relatively wealthy people are moving in from towns and cities, while the children of long-term residents are leaving rural areas to find work and homes they can afford. As a consequence, rural populations are, on average, slightly older than their urban counterparts. Increased mobility, combined with a decline in local shared facilities and wider societal trends, threatens community spirit. Stress is increasing, notably in the farming community. Some types of crime are increasing. Social exclusion in rural areas is often 'hidden' rather than absent – of particular concern are the elderly poor. Many rural people cannot afford to buy homes locally, and there is a shortage of social housing. Access to basic services remains a key problem for many.

People and places

Population

The population of rural areas has changed in recent years, both in numbers and content.

- Between 1984 and 1998, **the population of districts with a predominantly rural character[19] grew appreciably faster (10.3%) than that of England as a whole (5.3%)** (Figure 3.1).
- This increase is due, primarily, to net in-migration. However, out-migration from rural areas, mostly of younger people, has continued. As a result, **people in rural areas tend to be older, on average, than in the rest of the country** (Figure 3.2).

The proportion of the population living in rural England depends on how rural is defined.

- On the basis of ONS mid-year population estimates for 1998, some 28% of the population lived in districts of a predominantly rural character[19] (see Figure 3.1). A number of these districts incorporate towns, some of which have populations greater than the commonly accepted rurality threshold of 10,000.
- Researchers at Birkbeck College (SERRL) estimated that about 23% of the English population lives in rural areas. This estimate is based on census data for the proportion of people living in settlements of less than 10,000 and in non-urban areas, projected forward to 1998/99 on the basis of population growth estimates (J Shepherd, personal communication, 2000).

19. As defined by the former RDC and adopted in this report (see Page 4 and map on Page 65).

Figure 3.1 The proportion of the population of England living in predominantly rural districts, 1984 –1998

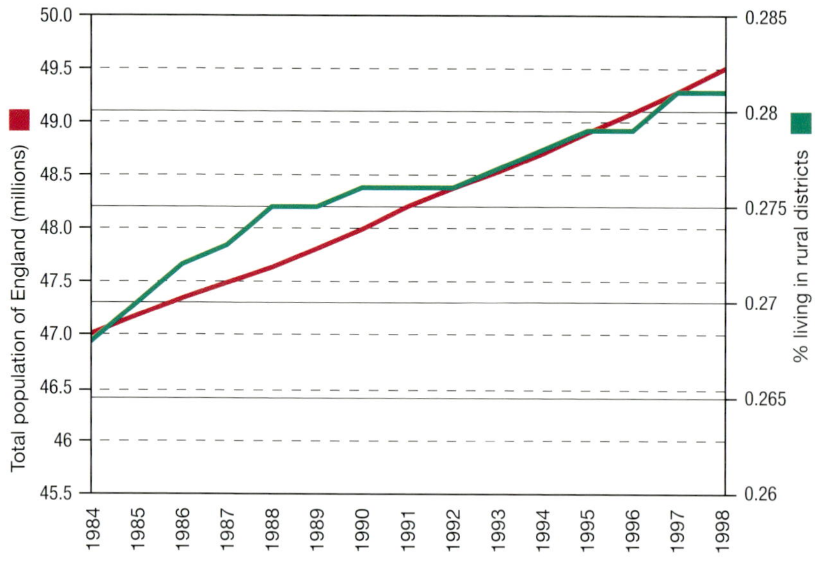

Source: Adapted from data provided by ONS Populations Estimates Unit

Figure 3.2 Comparison of the age structure of the populations of predominantly rural districts and other districts of England, 1998

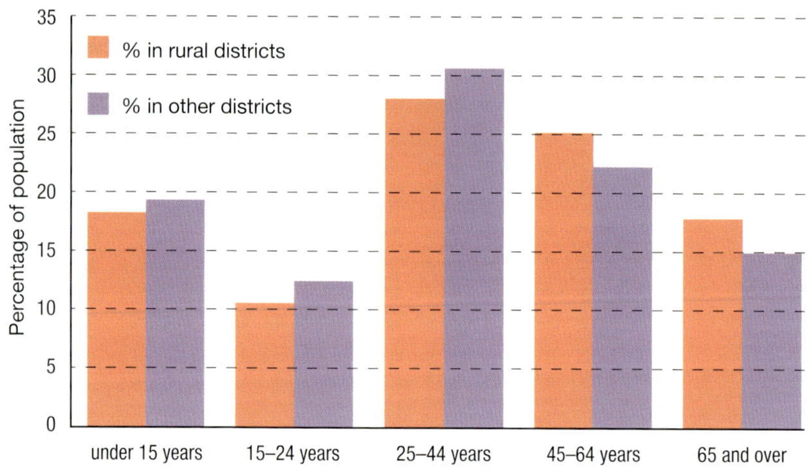

Source: Adapted from ONS Mid-Year Population Estimates – data provided by Nomis (Crown Copyright) December 1999

Incomers are a central feature of the rural scene (though by no means a new one[20]), and **both in-migration and out-migration are key factors of change affecting not only rural populations, but also the character of rural society and rural economies.** Recent research (Findlay *et al*, 1999; Winter *et al*, 1999) suggests that:

- There is a net inflow to rural areas of active, well-educated people, who on-average have higher incomes and are younger than the long-term residents. They move for 'employment' and 'quality of life' reasons.[21]

20. Eg. H J Massingham, writing in 1939, lamented the influx of 'week-enders' and the dispossession of 'native villagers', tracing back the phenomenon to the speculation by the early Tudor courtiers in the lands of village communities for conversion to sheep walks (Massingham, 1939).

21. There were, however, noticeable differences between the areas surveyed by Findlay et al (1999) with a distinct typology emerging. 'Commuter areas' (eg. South Warwickshire, Kent) reflect the above pattern most closely. 'Retirement areas' (eg. East Devon) are characterised by greater in-migration from outside the region, but with many incomers not working. In 'remote rural areas' (eg. Alnwick District), local and within-region movement predominates, with many working locally. Movement in 'older industrial areas' (eg. Wear Valley) is likely to be local or within the region; many work locally or are unemployed. These areas are the most likely to experience net out-migration.

- Out-migrants from rural areas are more likely to be young (ie. under 25), and to be moving for employment, education or personal reasons (eg. marriage or divorce).[22]

Settlements

There are over 16,500 settlements with populations of 10,000 and under in England (Figure 3.3); 13,148 of these have populations of less than 500 (the distribution of these, by district, is shown in Figure 3.4). However, some 6 million people live in settlements of 1,000 to 10,000.

Figure 3.3 Numbers and populations of small settlements

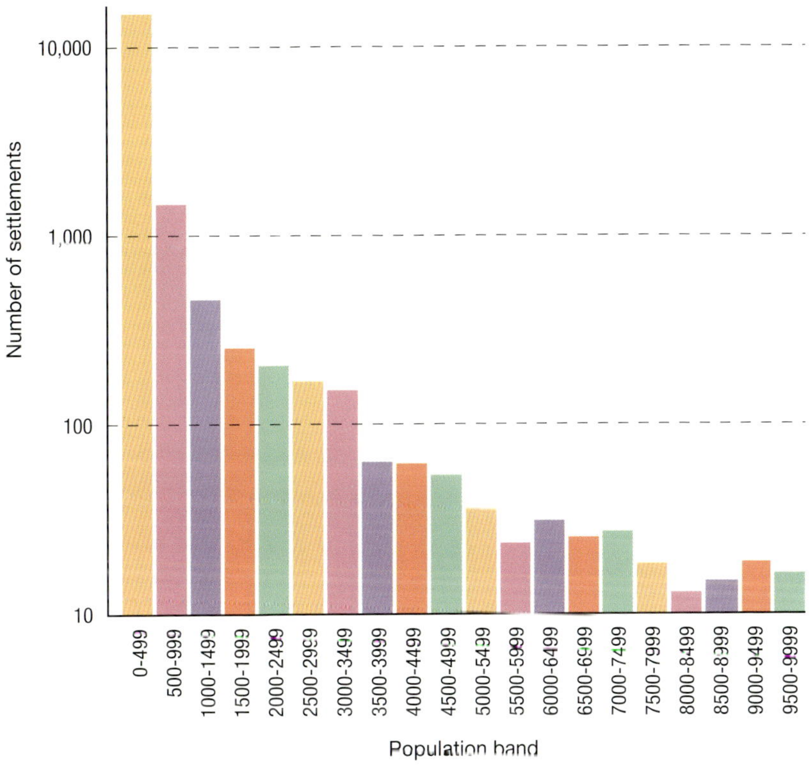

Source: RDC and Housing Corporation (1997)

22. The survey of Findlay et al (1999) concluded that the majority (84%) of out-migrants were the son or daughter of the head of household, with 73% aged under 25.

Figure 3.4 Proportion of households in settlements of less than 500 people, by district

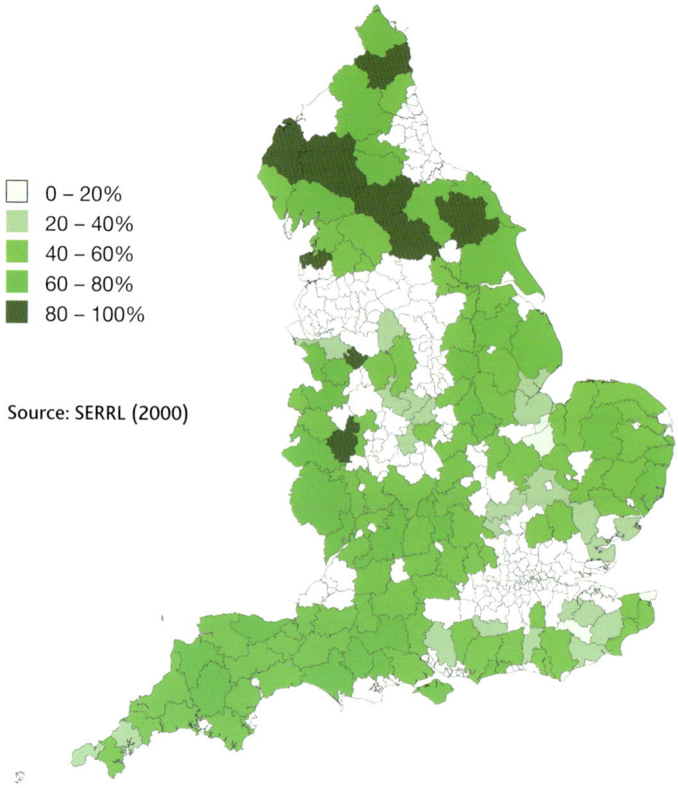

Source: SERRL (2000)

Cohesion and participation

Stronger and safer communities

Rural communities are widely perceived to be more cohesive, friendlier and safer than their urban counterparts. Of the people questioned in the 1999 British Social Attitudes Survey (who were drawn from all types of area):

- 65% agreed that there was 'more community spirit in the countryside';
- 72% felt 'the countryside is a better place to bring up children';
- 60% believed 'there is less crime in the countryside'.[23]

However, recent studies and surveys have identified that **there are a number of threats to community spirit and social cohesion in rural areas** (Bradley, 1987; Hedges, 1999; Jones, 2000; Palmer, 2000; Shucksmith, 1999; Winter *et al*, 1999) including:

- increased mobility and rapid population change;
- more people commuting instead of working in the community;
- decline of local shared facilities, such as shops, schools and pubs;
- increasingly individualistic lifestyles;
- loss of distinctive rural culture, language and dialects, and other intangible qualities;
- a possible weakening of links between market towns and surrounding villages and farms;[24]

23. Other recent surveys corroborate these findings:
– In the 1997 Survey of English Households, 68% of rural households said 'there is a lot of community spirit' in their area, compared with only 43% of urban households (with positive reporting of community spirit increasing with decreasing settlement size), while 47% of rural households said the people in their area were 'very friendly', compared with 34% of urban households (Hedges, 1999).
– A 1998 survey of 599 households in five contrasting rural areas of England reported 83% of respondents as 'satisfied' or 'highly satisfied' with the community spirit of their area (Findlay et al, 1999).

24. A recent analysis (Jones, 2000), based on 'extensive discussions with people in different parts of England', concluded that 'there are no longer strong ties of work, leisure and family that bonded towns to their surrounding villages and the farming community' and that 'country dwellers have developed more links with distant towns and many now skip the local centre altogether'. The author sees these as key factors in the fragmentation of formerly cohesive rural communities consisting of farmsteads, villages and market towns.

- conflicts between incomers, and locals and farmers;[25]
- loss of younger people.[26]

25. In the questionnaire survey of Winter et al (1999), 59% of locals and 52% of incomers agreed that new conflicts were arising between incomers and locals; incomer-farmer conflicts were referred to by 39% of locals and 30% of incomers. There was considerable variation between the five study areas (in Cheshire, Devon, Hampshire, Norfolk and Powys): the proportion of local respondents identifying incomer-local conflicts ranged from 45% in Cheshire to 78% in Norfolk; farmer-incomer conflicts were mentioned by 52% of Norfolk locals, but only 23% of Hampshire locals.

26. Among other effects, the loss of younger people can 'inhibit the social reproduction of the community and damage informal support networks'. In particular, the elderly may become socially isolated as their children are priced out of local housing markets (Bradley, 1987; JRF, 1999; Shucksmith, 1999).

Social places

There are approximately 8,900 village halls and similar community buildings in rural England (excluding churches) (Beaton, 1998):

- 75% are the only community facility in their village.
- Over half are more than 60 years old.
- 86% are run as charities.

Rural pubs, shops, schools etc all provide important social focis beyond their central service role. Where these are closing (see Pages 30–35), there will be consequences not only for service provision, but also for community cohesion.

Community activities

Rural people participate in a range of activities, as shown in Figure 3.5.

Figure 3.5 Community activities in rural areas, 1997

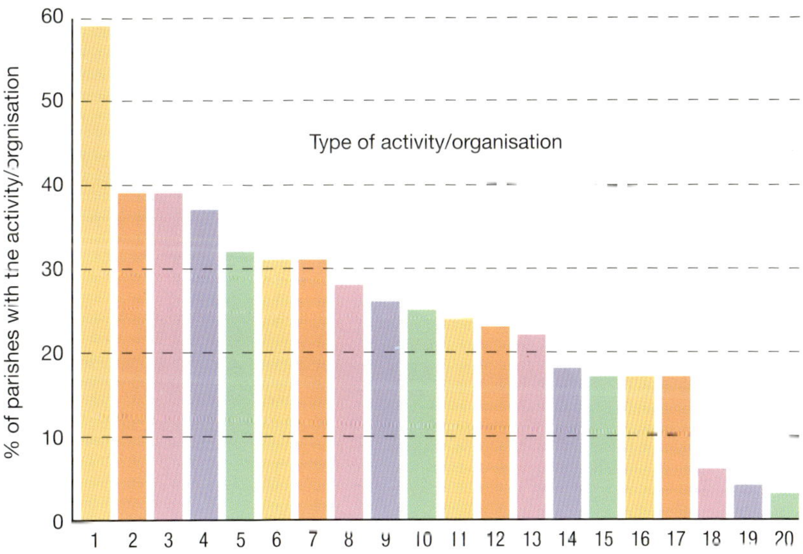

1 Women's Institute/Mothers' Union
2 Football clubs
3 Recreational clubs for older people
4 cricket clubs
5 Youth clubs/other young peoples' clubs
6 Rainbows/Brownies/Guides/Rangers
7 Keep fit clubs
8 Bowls clubs
9 Beavers/Cubs/Scouts/Venture scouts
10 Gardening clubs
11 Other miscellaneous recreational groups
12 Other women's recreational groups
13 Dancing clubs
14 Music groups/societies
15 Badminton clubs
16 Tennis clubs
17 British Legion
18 Young farmers' clubs
19 Rugby clubs
20 Swimming clubs

Source: RDC (1997)

A recent survey (Findlay *et al*, 1999) concluded that households that move from an urban location, that have higher incomes and that commute to work beyond the immediate area, are more actively involved in local community activities than other movers.[27] While there was little evidence, from this survey, that incomers 'take over the running of local affairs', Winter *et al* (1999), identified some antipathy towards incomers who were seen as wanting to 'take charge and alter things'.

27. For incomers to rural areas, lacking local roots, participation may be an important means of belonging or demonstrating their commitment to the local community. In contrast, established rural people's sense of belonging derives from long-term residence, family continuity, dialect and a confidence in being country people (Derounian, 1993).

Rural churches

Churches have been at the heart of rural life for centuries. Church numbers and attendance have, however, declined in general, with sample surveys[28] in 1989 and 1998 suggesting that rural areas have been disproportionally affected. According to these surveys, between 1989 and 1998 (see Figure 3.6):

- the total number of extant churches declined by 0.6% in urban areas, and 4.6% in rural areas;
- the numbers of people attending church regularly on Sundays declined by nearly 17% in urban areas, and nearly 40% in rural areas.[29]

However, the churches, taken together, represent a significant presence and resource (in terms of members, ministers and buildings) in rural England, and **churches play an important role in many rural communities.**

- Church buildings are often noted landmarks in village centres; many have great historical and aesthetic value.[30]
- There are many more churches in rural areas per head of population than in non-rural areas.[31]
- The church hall often provides a venue for a variety of community groups as well as groups provided or supported by the church itself.
- The church noticeboard and newsletter are important, and may be the only, sources of written local information.[32]
- Many rural primary schools are church schools (usually aided or controlled by the local education authority).

Figure 3.6 Estimated numbers of churches and Sunday attendance by environment[33], England, 1989–1998

	Urban	Rural	Total
1989			
Numbers of churches	22,006	16,601	38,607
Sunday attendance	3,699,384	1,043,416	4,742,800
1998			
Numbers of churches	21,876	15,841	37,717
Sunday attendance	3,083,201	631,499	3,714,700

Sources: Derived from the English Church Census 1989 (MARC Europe) and the English Church Attendance Survey 1998 (Christian Research).

Local action

Village or parish appraisals are a means of taking stock of a community as a basis for future action. They, hence, promote participation in governance and enhance empowerment.

- **By 1997, some 1,200 parish appraisals had been undertaken, involving up to 15,000 local people** (Moseley, 1997).

28. The English Church Census 1989 by MARC Europe and the English Church Attendance Survey 1998 by Christian Research (see Brierley, 1999, 2000). In both cases, all known churches were sent questionnaires: c 70% responded in 1989, c 33% in 1998. Attendance in 1989 was as counted on a specified Sunday; in 1998, it was gauged by average number on a typical Sunday in September'. In 1998, church 'environment' was not directly collected, but derived from data collected in 1989.

29. The observed drop in (regular) Sunday attendance partly reflects the reduced frequency of Sunday services in many rural parishes.

30. Of the Church of England's 1998 stock of some 18 400 churches, just over 10,000 are listed buildings; of these an estimated 5,000 are rural Norman churches. A regional analysis of the English Church Attendance Survey 1998 indicated that the highest proportion of listed churches is in the (predominantly rural) South-West and East-Anglia regions (Brierley, 1999, 2000).

31. An approximate indication of this is provided by comparing the estimated proportion of churches (42%) in rural areas in 1998 (Figure 3.5) and the population (27%) in rural districts (Figure 3.1). Sample surveys between 1988 and 1996 of different types of rural area estimated the ratio of inhabitants to churches as follows: remote or marginal countryside – 175; less accessible countryside – 270; accessible countryside – 700; urban shadow countryside – 800 (Francis, 1996).

32. In 1996, some 74% of rural parishes had a church newsletter; 45% had a village newsletter; and 93% had at least one public noticeboard (RDC, 1997).

33. Church 'environment' is as assessed by respondents. 'Urban' is an amalgamation of 'city centre', 'inner city', 'council estate', 'suburban/urban fringe', 'separate town' and 'other built-up area' categories. 'Rural' is an amalgamation of 'rural: commuter dormitory' and 'rural: other areas' categories.

- Surveys in two English counties in 1990–93 showed an average community response of 74% (Moseley *et al*, 1996).[34]

Village design statements enable residents to assess the character of their village and express their views as to how any development should proceed, in order to protect or enhance that character.

- By 1998, at least 176 villages across England had produced or were producing village design statements (W S Atkins, 1998).

Community audits[35] help organise and motivate local people, while making the most of local distinctiveness. A combination of Rapid Rural Appraisal, meetings and questionnaires results in a five-year community development action plan that is implemented by the community and relevant agencies.

- By 1997, some 20 community audits had been completed, with several positive impacts on both communities and external organisations (Pretty, 1998).

Parish maps[36] involve the production of a local map by local people that reflects a wide range of viewpoints. Environmental concerns and historical interest often feature highly. The maps provide a focus for working together and developing a common sense of community, as well as a basis for addressing local concerns.

Health

Basic health indicators, such as low birth weights, mortality, death under 65, limiting long-term illness, and suicide (Figure 3.7), suggest that, **overall, rural people are as healthy as or healthier than their urban counterparts.**

Figure 3.7 Comparison of basic health indicators for rural and non-rural England

	Rural	Non-rural
Low birth weight (% babies born with low birthweight 1991–98)	8	7
Mortality (deaths per 100,000 population 1991–98)	701	765
Premature death (deaths under 65 per 100,000 population 1991–98)	200	234
Long-term illness (% residents with long-term illness 1991)	11.90	13.15
Suicide (average suicide rate per 100,000 population 1991–98)	9	10

Source: Adapted from data provided by ONS Populations Estimates Unit.

34. Impacts of successful village appraisals include:
– Increased confidence and cohesion among local people.
– Increased motivation amongst parish councils to take action on local issues.
– The emergence of new groups, especially for young people.
– Greater likelihood of external agencies acting on local plans.
– Benefits for external organisations, including better information to target resources.
However, recommended action points from village appraisals are much more likely to be implemented if this can be achieved by local people alone, than if action by external agencies is required. Despite the participatory process, it still appears difficult for local communities to effect changes to education, jobs, policing, healthcare and low-cost housing, even if they have been identified as important (Pretty, 1998).

35. Community audits were developed originally for the district of North Kesteven, Lincolnshire (Kelly, 1997).

36. Parish maps have been developed and promoted by the charity, Common Ground (Clifford, 1997).

These broad-based statistics, however, cover only some aspects of health and conceal appreciable variations between different areas and within rural communities. For example, health is poor in rural coalfield areas and occupational health risks are high among farmers and farm workers.

Rising levels of stress in the farming community have been observed in England (along with most countries of the western world) (Monk, 1999).[37] In response to this, several caring agencies have developed rural outreach initiatives[38] and a number of new organisations have been formed.[39]

Crime

Absolute risks of crime in rural districts are in most respects lower than in most urban areas, as indicated by an analysis of the British Crime Survey 1996 (for England and Wales) (Mirlees-Black, 1998).[40]

- In 1995, 3.9% of rural households were burgled, compared with 6.3% in urban areas and 10.3% in inner-city areas. Risks of vandalism, burglary and vehicle-related thefts were also lower for retail and manufacturing premises in rural locations.
- People living in rural areas are less concerned about falling victim to crime than those living in other parts of the country, and feel safer on their local streets.[41]
- Public confidence in the police is higher in rural areas than elsewhere, as is satisfaction with the service provided by the police to victims reporting crimes.

However, **some types of crime have increased in rural areas at a rate greater than elsewhere** (Mirlees-Black, 1998).

- From 1991 to 1995, vehicle-related thefts increased by 24% in rural areas, compared with 4% in urban areas and 10% in inner cities.
- Between 1991 and 1995, contact crime increased by 60% in rural areas, 48% in urban areas and 91% in inner-city areas.
- In rural areas a higher proportion of burglaries result in entry to the property and theft.

Social exclusion

Social exclusion is multi-dimensional, describing what happens when people are unable to participate in the civic, social, economic and cultural opportunities that most take for granted. It incorporates a range of experiences, relating, for example, to income and poverty, education, employment, health, housing, access to services, and relationships within families and with the wider community.

Social exclusion is ubiquitous, but there are aspects that are particular to rural areas.[42]

37. According to surveys by the NFU (1999, 2000), many farmers experienced 'classic symptoms of stress' while 1 in 10 tenant farmers were said to be taking anti-depressants. According to Hawton et al (1998), farmers are also a 'high-risk-from-suicide' occupational group,with a 1991-1996 proportional mortality ratio (PMR) from suicide of 144 (against a population standard of 100).

38. Eg. The Samaritans launched their Rural Outreach Initiative in 1987 and are active partners in most county initiatives. Citizens' Advice Bureaux have also been partners in many such initiatives. In 1998, the Royal Agricultural Benevolent Institution (RABI) launched an emergency appeal and, as a consequence, has helped about 234 farmers and their families with a total of £230,000 (C Davies, personal communication, 2000).

39. Eg. Rural Stress Information Network, Farm Crisis Network and the Shropshire Rural Stress Support Network. There are also now 28 County Rural Support Groups in England with 'card schemes', publicising organisations that help rural people in distress (C Davies, personal communication, 2000).

40. Rural areas were defined as falling into Acorn types 1–9 and 27. The Acorn system is a geodemographic targeting system built entirely using census data. A combination of demographic and socio-economic variables is used to classify people into one of 54 types (CACI, 1999).

41. There is some conflicting evidence of a belief that crime is rising in rural areas and a sense of heightened vulnerability, especially to property crime committed by people from outside the immediate area (Anderson, 1999; Hedges, 1999). Fear of crime is exacerbated by community fragmentation and reduced social cohesion, and awareness of increasingly stretched police resources and decreased scope for traditional policing methods.

42. See also sections on health (p 25), housing (p 27), services (p 30) and employment (p 37).

- **Socially excluded households in rural areas tend to be geographically dispersed**; urban social exclusion is often concentrated, especially on housing estates.[43]
- Rural social exclusion differs from that in urban areas in content and character (eg. rural housing problems relate more to affordability than quality).
- **Poor access to jobs, services etc, due to distances and isolation, transport costs and limited public transport, are far bigger issues for rural than for urban people.**[44]
- The myth of the rural idyll means that many people find it hard to accept that social exclusion can exist in pleasant surroundings. Rural people may be more independently minded and self-reliant and less able or willing to recognise or declare need.
- Rural areas are often places of extremes, with some of the richest people living alongside some of the poorest.[45] While many rural elderly have retired there with substantial wealth, others among **the elderly constitute the largest low-income social grouping in rural areas.**[46]
- Other low-income groups characteristic of rural areas are: low-paid, manual workers' households (notably working in agriculture or tourism); those detached from labour markets (ie unemployed, early retired, long-term sick or disabled); and self-employed people (23% of those of working age on low incomes in rural Britain) (Shucksmith, 1999).[47]

The Government's Index of Local Deprivation (ILD) 1998 placed five rural districts[48] (DETR, 1998c) amongst the one hundred most deprived areas; this despite this Index's acknowledged weakness at picking up deprivation of the type and dispersed nature found in rural areas.

Housing

Stock and projected need

There were nearly 4 million dwellings in rural England in 1996 (20% of England's total housing stock) (Countryside Agency, 1999d); 5% of these had been built since 1991 (compared to 3% in urban areas).

The number of households in rural districts of England is projected to increase by more than one million (ie 19%) from 1996 to 2016[49] (King, 2000).

- This increase will arise more or less equally from household formation by the existing rural population and from inward migration.
- Most of the rural increase (70%) will be one-person households, some created from current multiple person households (RDC, 1998a).

43. This makes rural social exclusion much more difficult to locate and address through area- or regionally based policies or community development.

44. In most rural areas, a car is a necessity and not necessarily a sign of relative affluence or advantage.

45. For example, according to Gomm (1997), some 27% of all households in Cotswold District had annual incomes of less than £7,000, while 33% had incomes in excess of £25,000.

46. Predominantly widows, the poor rural elderly are often wholly reliant on the state pension and are affected by disadvantages such as isolation and poor access to services. In many cases, their children, unable to find work or afford housing locally, will have moved away.

47. Low income and poverty are key aspects of social exclusion:
– Studies in rural England in 1979 and 1990 found 1 in 4 rural households living in or on the margins of poverty (cited by Shucksmith, 1999).
– A study of 7,000 individuals from 1991 – 1996 from both rural and non-rural areas of Great Britain concluded that proportionately fewer individuals received low incomes in rural areas and spells of low income were shorter. However, 1 in 3 individuals in rural Britain experienced at least one spell of poverty in this five-year period, and the differences in incidence of poverty between rural and non-rural areas were small (Chapman et al, 1998).
– Research in 12 contrasting rural areas found that in 9 of them over 23% of households were below the poverty threshold of half average income (Cloke et al, 1994, 1995).

48. Wear Valley, Penwith, Kerrier, Thanet and Pendle.

49. 'Rural' districts are defined by inclusion in shire counties which have at least one district which is RDC-defined as 'rural'.

Condition

Houses in rural areas are generally in better condition than in urban areas (DETR, 1998a):

- 5% of rural homes are unfit for human habitation, compared to 8% of urban dwellings.
- 10% of rural households are accommodated in poor housing, compared to 15% of urban households.

Second homes and vacant homes

In 1991 some **58% (46,932) of England's second homes were located in rural districts.**

- However, even in rural areas, a low percentage of homes were second homes (0.9%, compared to 0.4% nationally) (ONS Census of Population Statistics 1991 – NOMIS (Crown Copyright) January 2000).
- A lower proportion of rural homes (3.5%) are vacant than is the case in urban areas (4.1%) (Countryside Agency, 1999d).
- There is considerable regional variation, with much higher than average proportions of second homes in popular holiday areas.

Tenure

There was, in 1996, more owner-occupied housing (74%) and less council/housing association tenanted housing (15%) in rural areas than in England as whole (67% and 23% respectively) (Countryside Agency, 1999d).

Affordable housing

Many rural people are unable to buy their own houses locally, while there is a shortage of affordable housing[50] and private rented housing.

- A key factor contributing to the shortage of rural affordable housing is the prosperous incomer bidding up the rural housing market beyond the reach of long-term rural dwellers.[51]
- The supply of local authority rented housing, which has always been limited in rural areas, was severely depleted during the 1980s, mostly as a result of the 'Right to Buy' legislation, and has not been matched by the provision of new units.[52]

There are major obstacles to replacing the losses of local authority housing and meeting arising needs (ACRE, 1993; DTZ Pieda, 1998; RDC, 1995, 1996).

- Rural housing needs are often poorly identified in official statistics and often left unaddressed in local authority and regional planning guidance.

50. Affordable housing is defined as housing made available to people who cannot afford to purchase properties that are generally available on the open market. Such housing can be for rent or part-owned on a shared equity basis. It may also be 'low-cost' market housing (DETR, 1998b).

51. The survey of Findlay et al (1999) in five contrasting rural areas confirmed the stereotypical view of the 'prosperous incomer bidding up the housing market beyond the reach of long-term locals', and revealed a clear gap between incomers and local movers in the level of attainment of owner-occupation. Earlier research (Bramley, 1995) concluded that, in 1991, 40% of newly forming households in rural areas would be unable to enter the owner-occupied housing market

52. From 1985 to 1990, 91,000 homes were lost from the local authority rented sector in rural districts; from 1991 to 1997, only 17,000 new units were provided. To safeguard affordable housing in rural areas, the 1996 Housing Act now exempts new affordable housing schemes in villages of less than 3,000 population from the 'Right to Buy'.

- There is a shortage of sites available at viable prices and a lack of public funding to support provision. Local opposition to schemes often leads to delay.

Most new affordable housing is provided through Registered Social Landlords funded from the Housing Corporation's Rural Programme.

- Between 1993/94 and 1999/2000 the number of units approved through the Housing Corporation Rural Development Programme fell from 1,618 to 800. The rural allocation for 2000/01 is 750 units (Housing Corporation, 1999; personal communication 2000).
- The proportional rural target (3.4% in 1998) has remained relatively stable during the last 10 years, but because the Housing Corporation Approved Development Programme has been cut during the same period, the number of units achieved through the Rural Programme declined (Housing Corporation, personal communication 2000).
- In 1998/1999, 218 local authorities defined as 'rural' by the Housing Corporation did not receive any grant from the Corporation's Rural Programme.[53]

Rural schemes are often more expensive to develop, but this is not reflected in the proportion of Housing Corporation funding going to rural schemes. In 1997/98 the national headline grant rate was 54%, but, on average, rural schemes only received 35%. The Housing Corporation has introduced a rural multiplier to reflect the higher costs of developing small schemes in villages, but this does not make up for the shortfall arising from low grant rates.

Rural homelessness

Homelessness in rural areas is increasing, but has a much lower national profile than its urban counterpart (Cloke *et al*, 2000).[54]

- In the early 1990s, around 16,000 families in rural districts were accepted as priority homeless each year (about 12% of the national total) (RDC, 1993).
- Between 1992 and 1996, rural homelessness rose from 11.8% to 14.4%. In some rural districts, the increases were particularly dramatic, with 8 districts noting rises of more than 50%.[55] In contrast, homelessness in London and urban local authorities fell by 27.3% and 17.6% respectively (Cloke *et al*, 2000).

The full extent of rural homelessness, particularly among young people, is often hidden, and the problems of those facing homelessness are exacerbated by a lack of emergency accommodation and accessible advice. The reduction in local authority stock has weakened their ability to tackle the issue, while problems of availability, accessibility and affordability prevent many households from entering the private rented sector.

53. The Housing Corporation's definition of a rural local authority is not synonymous with that of the Countryside Agency. The Housing Corporation's Rural Programme provides funding for schemes in settlements of less than 3,000 population

54. In general, most homelessness acceptances arise from: loss of private rented or tied accommodation; parents or other relatives no longer willing to accommodate a household, relationship breakdown with a partner; mortgage arrears. The main causes of homelessness in rural areas are mortgage arrears and the loss of private rented housing (Cloke et al, 2000).

55. Ie. Isles of Scilly, South Hampshire, Daventry, Forest of Dean, Richmondshire, South Shropshire, Selby and North Dorset.

Services

Most people regard easy access to GP surgeries, corner shops, supermarkets and public transport, for example, as important[56], but people in rural areas do not find it as easy to get to many basic services as do people in urban areas[57]. However, in many rural areas, **local services are declining and accessing basic services can be difficult** (Countryside Agency, 1999c).

- In both 'lone-shop' villages and small town centres, **many smaller food shops are only marginally viable, while some have already closed.**
- **Post offices continue to decline in numbers**[58], with some indications that the greatest losses have been in the more remote rural districts (Figure 3.8).
- **Rural pubs are declining at an estimated average rate of around 3 per county per year.**
- **Traditional branch GP surgeries continue to close, NHS dental practices are declining, and small town pharmacies face growing competition** from superstores and other outlets.
- **Pre-school and out-of-school childcare provision has grown, but remains patchy and difficult to access for some.**

In contrast, **rural primary schools appear at present to be relatively stable, with few threats of closure and rising educational standards** as evidenced by generally favourable Ofsted reports. School rolls, however, appear more volatile with overcrowding in some schools and surplus places in others possibly as the result of parental preference and localised demographic change. In recent years, a number of village halls have been successful in raising funds from a range of sources for refurbishment and upgrading (Countryside Agency, 1999c).

Patterns of access to services vary appreciably across the country.

- In terms of access to post offices, many of the less well-served districts are in the North and Midlands. In the East Riding, 21% of households live further than 1 km from a post office; the corresponding figure for Herefordshire is 31%. In contrast, in many parts of the South, almost 100% of households have a post office within 1 km (Figure 3.9).
- Access to pubs relates strongly to proximity to urban areas. In East Hertfordshire, for example, only 4% of households are more than 1 km from a pub; corresponding figures for mid-Suffolk and Ryedale (North Yorks.) are 21% and 50% (Figure 3.10).
- GP surgeries are most accessible in or around urban areas: for example, only 3% of households in Tandridge (Surrey) are more than 5 km from a surgery. The proportion rises with increasing 'rurality', but only gently. In Breckland (Norfolk) 13% of households fall outside this threshold of service; in West Devon, the comparable figure is 18% (Figure 3.11).

56. Eg. Between 60% and 80% of people questioned in the 1999 British Social Attitudes Survey regarded it as 'fairly important' or 'very important' that these services were 'within a 15 minute walk away'.

57. Eg. The 1997 Survey of English Housing revealed that a lower proportion of rural households than of urban households found it 'very easy' to get to corner shops (73% compared with 81%) and supermarkets (54% compared with 65%); ease of access to post offices, however, appeared more or less the same for rural and urban households (Hedges, 1999).

58. Rural post offices are threatened by: the loss of the 'benefits and bills business' (which are increasingly paid by bank transfer and direct debit); fear of burglary or armed robbery; and the sale of stamps at other outlets.

Figure 3.8 Net change in numbers of post offices, 1995–1999, by district

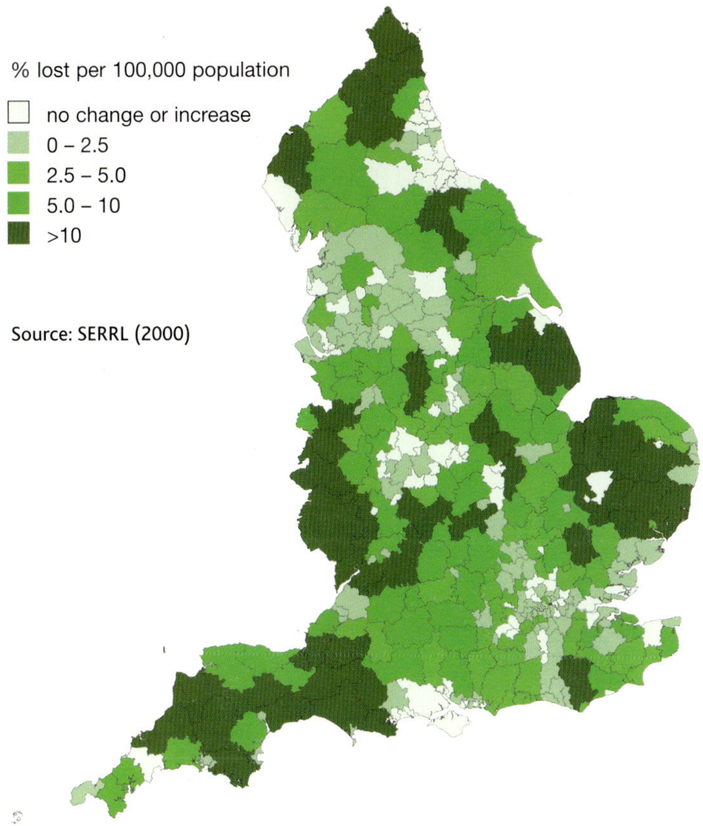

Source: SERRL (2000)

Figure 3.9 Proportion (%) of households more than 1 km from a post office, by district

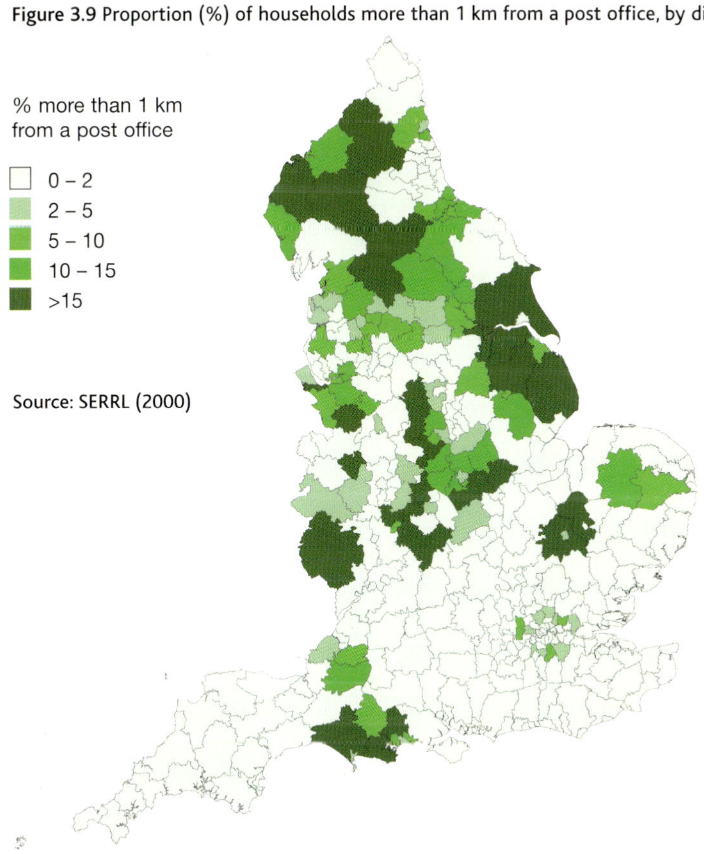

Source: SERRL (2000)

Figure 3.10 Proportion (%) of households more than 1 km from a pub, by district[59]

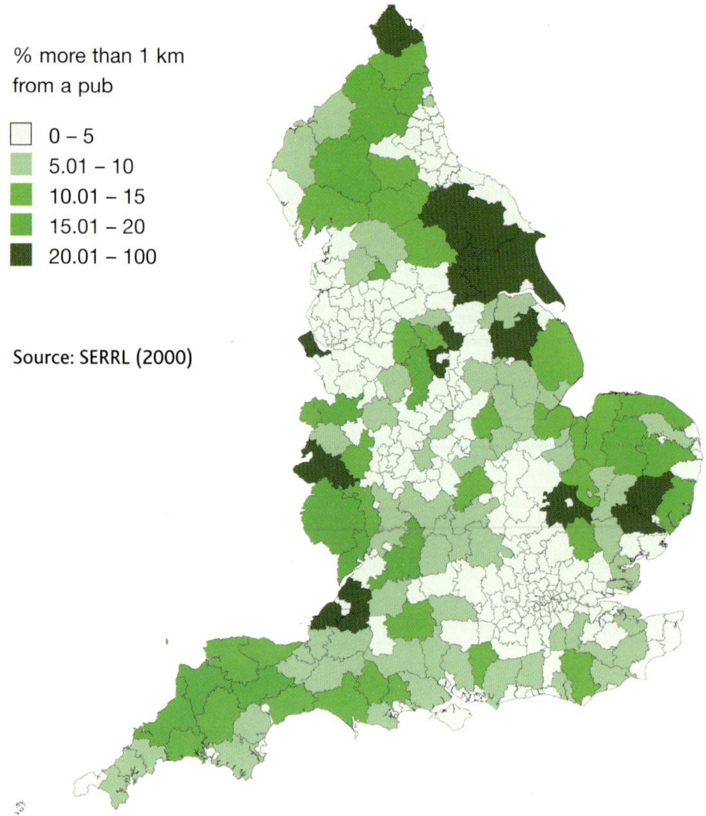

Source: SERRL (2000)

Figure 3.11 Proportion (%) households more than 5 km from a surgery, by district[60]

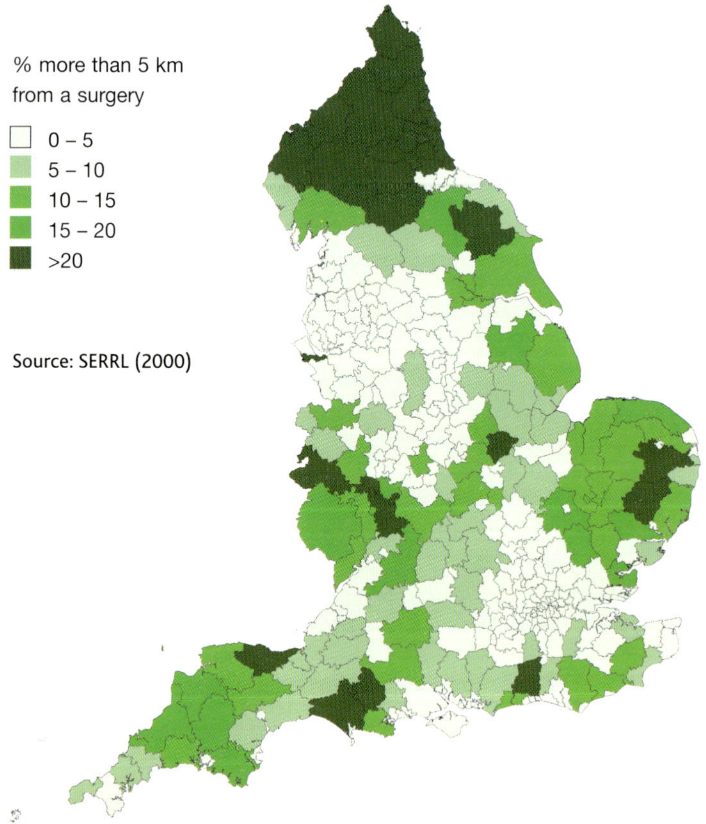

Source: SERRL (2000)

59. The apparent absence of pubs in the Wirral is due mostly to data not having been adjusted, as yet, by the Post Office, following changes in post-code allocations for the area.

60. The apparently very sparse distribution of surgeries in the North East is partly explained by the large number of group practices that use a single address point, even though they may have a number of branch surgeries.

- Access to hospitals shows greater variation than access to GP surgeries. For example, 46% of households in the East Riding and 29% in Torridge (Devon) are more than 10 km from a hospital. In Aylesbury (Bucks), by contrast, the corresponding value is 2% (Figure 3.12).
- Differences in levels of access to primary schools are also pronounced. In Eden (Cumbria), one of the more remote rural districts, 41% of households are more than 2 km from a primary school. In Waverley (Surrey) and Hinckley (Leicestershire), in different regions, but both close to urban centres, less than 1% of households fall in this category (Figure 3.13).
- Access to secondary schools, measured by the proportion of households living within 5 km of a school, shows a more complex pattern. In some rural areas, access levels are quite high. West Dorset has only 3% of households outside the threshold and West Oxfordshire only 8%. This contrasts sharply with East Lindsey (Lincolnshire), for example, where 80% of households are beyond 5 km of a school (Figure 3.14).

There are several approaches that have helped, or may help, to maintain local services.

- **Business Rate Relief.** Introduced in April 1998, this should help to reduce the overheads of village shops, and post offices.
- **Diversification.** Possibilities for traditional village food shops include video hire, tourist information, film processing, and franchises to sell lottery tickets. Pubs can market their premises as a wider community resource. The Post Office Horizon Initiative aims, through automation, to raise the level of service and generate new business.
- **Joint-service provision.** New post offices can be sited in village halls, pubs and farm shops. Several rural health centres and GP practices are providing a growing range of services, some involving the use of modern community centres and village halls as additional access points. There is a growing use of school premises for the wider community (eg for life-long learning and holiday use).
- **Partnerships.** Links between local growers and local food shops can help to maintain the viability of both sets of businesses. The clustering of small local schools to pool resources, and widen educational opportunities is common in some areas.
- **Local 'self-help'.** Some communities have bought, and now run, their local shop or pub. Community self-help in relation to health care is thriving in some places.[61] Many schools enjoy local community support through fund-raising, assistance with transport and help in the classroom(Countryside Agency, 1999c).

61. Eg. Befriending and after-care, local transport provision, new or alternative premises and fund-raising activities. There are also several examples across the country where repeat prescriptions are delivered to village post offices for ease of collection.

Fig 3.12 Proportion (%) of households more than 10 km from a hospital, by district

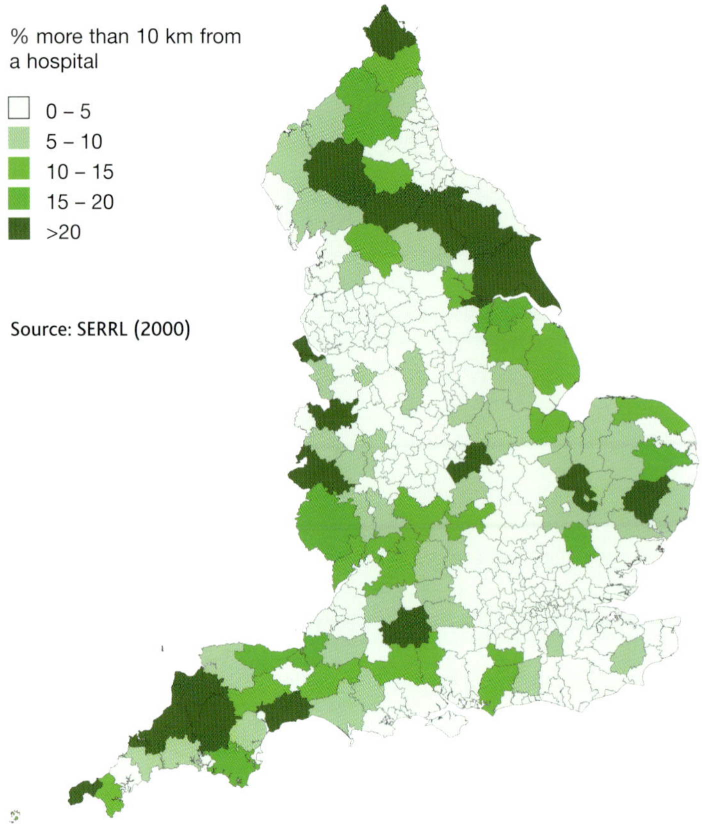

Source: SERRL (2000)

Figure 3.13 Proportion (%) of households more than 2 km from a primary school, by district

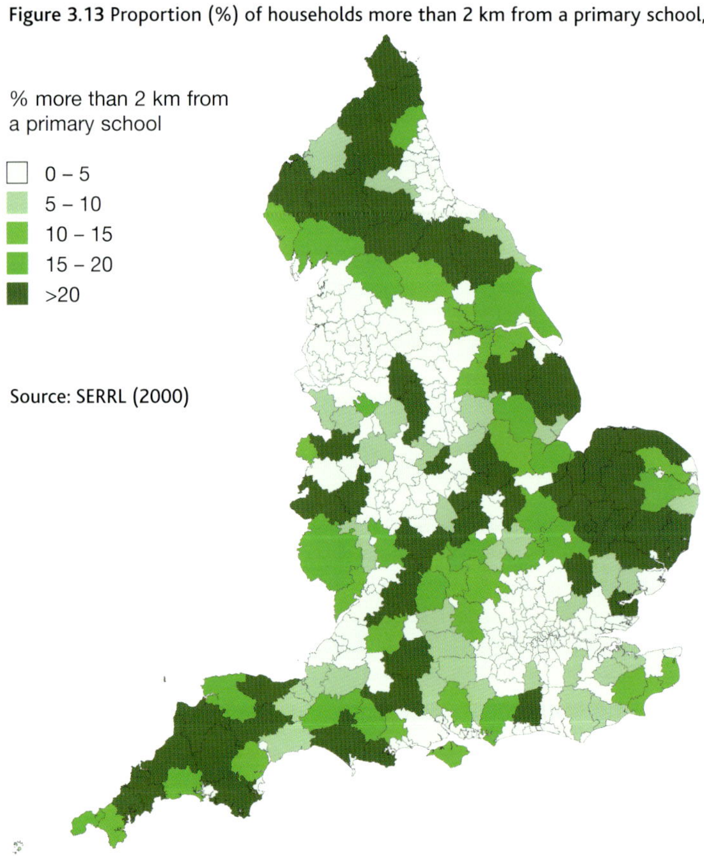

Source: SERRL (2000)

Figure 3.14 Proportion (%) of house holds more than 5 km from a secondary school, by district

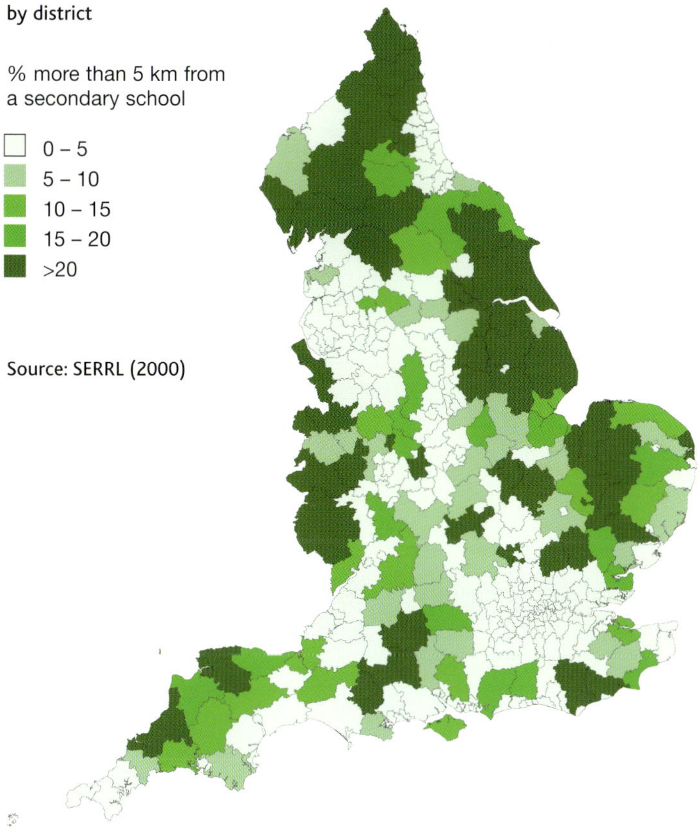

Source: SERRL (2000)

4 Economic opportunity with vibrant enterprise and sustainable agriculture

Mark Osborne/Countryside Agency

Farmers' market, Melksham, Wiltshire.

Employment and self-employment are higher in rural areas than urban areas and claimant unemployment lower. This might suggest rural people are prospering. However, average earnings are lower, including among the self-employed, and rural jobs are more likely to be part-time, casual or seasonal. Surveys point to higher levels of hidden unemployment in some rural areas. Getting to work can be a serious constraint for some.

Traditional employment in primary and land-based industries has declined, while the service sector has increased. There are several rural counties among the lowest in England in terms of GDP per head. Farm incomes and numbers of farms have declined, and average farm size has increased; farming's direct contribution to GDP has declined. Tourism has become important for rural economies and employment, though there are indications of a recent fall in numbers of tourists and in spending.

However, some of the changes in the countryside may be generating new jobs, for example, in nature conservation or in manufacture and marketing of speciality rural products. 'Incomers' may create new employment in rural areas. Organic farming is increasing, and has potential for further expansion (as well as contributing to sustainable development). Many farmers are recognising the need to diversify.

Employment

Patterns of employment

Districts of England of a predominantly rural character[62] have, on average, higher employment and self-employment and lower claimant unemployment than urban districts (Figures 4.1, 4.2, 4.3).

Figure 4.1 Employment in rural and other districts as a proportion of total population of working age, England 1992–1999

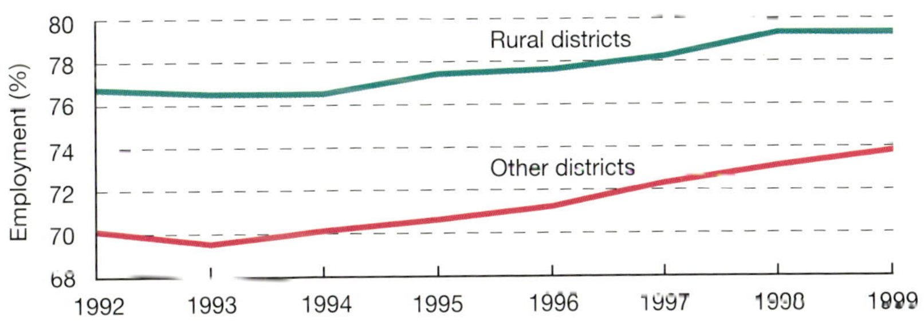

Source: ONS Labour Force Survey, NOMIS (Crown Copyright) January 2000

Figure 4.2 Self-employment in rural and other districts as a proportion of total population of working age, England 1992–1999[63]

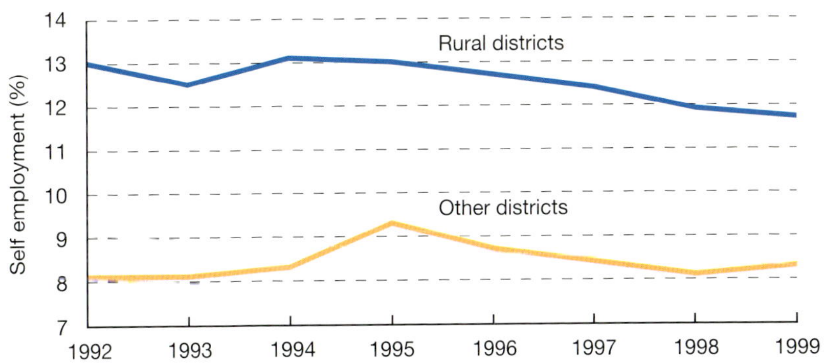

Source: ONS Labour Force Survey, NOMIS (Crown Copyright) January 2000

62. Ie. As defined by the former RDC and adapted in this report (see page 4 and map on page 65).

63. Self-employment varies considerably across the regions. For example self employed people accounted for over 23% of the total workforce in Cornwall in 1997, but only 8.2% in Durham in 1998 (compared with England at 13%) (TCPA, 1999).

Figure 4.3 Claimant unemployment in rural and other districts as a proportion of total population of working age, 1992–1999

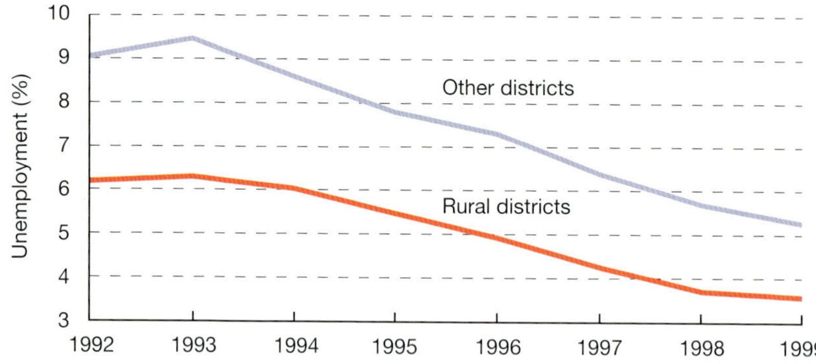

Source: ONS Labour Force Survey, NOMIS (Crown Copyright) January 2000

Rural areas have experienced change in the structure of employment and enterprise (Figures 4.4). The main features have been:

- **a decline in employment in agriculture, energy, water and construction;**
- **an increase in employment in the service sector,** notably in tourism, banking, finance and insurance, and public administration and education.

VAT registrations and deregistrations (Figure 4.5) also indicate a shift away from primary industries and towards services.

Figure 4.4 Employment in rural areas by sector, 1991–1997

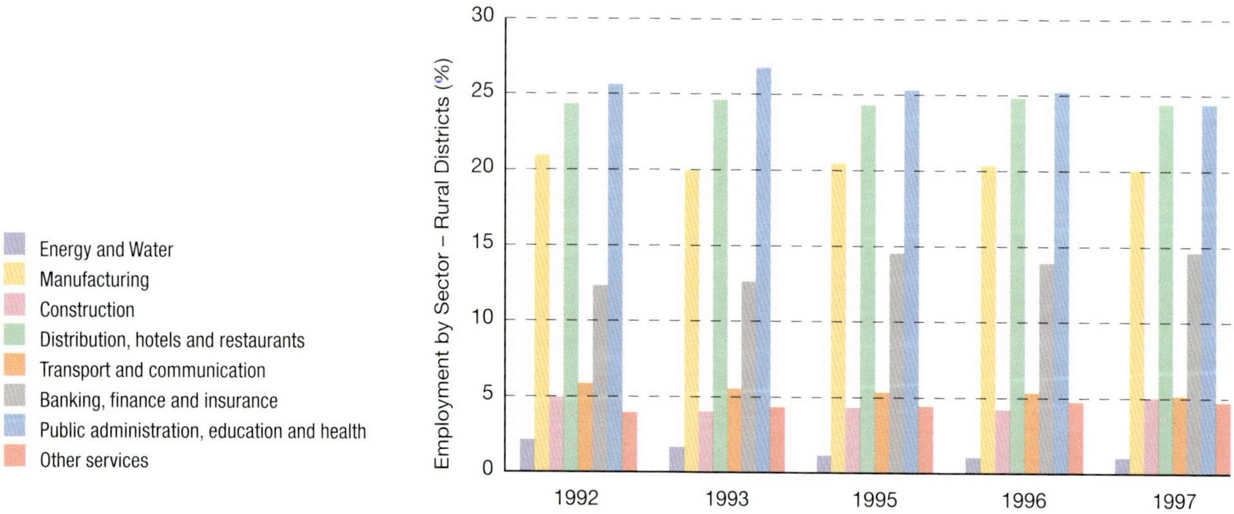

Source: ONS Census of Population, NOMIS (Crown Copyright) December 1999

Figure 4.5 VAT registrations in rural areas by sector, 1997–1998

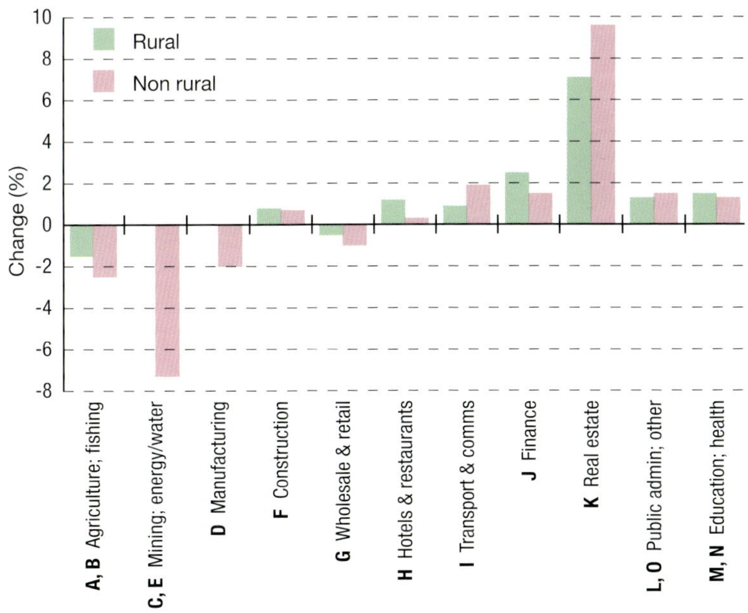

Source: DTI/ONS VAT registrations and deregistrations by Industry, NOMIS (Crown Copyright) December 1999

Employment disadvantage

Figures 4.1–4.3 conceal appreciable regional variations, and provide no indication of hidden unemployment[64], levels of earnings or employment quality.

- There are indications that **hidden unemployment is higher in some rural areas** (and by consequence real unemployment). Estimated real (ie. hidden+claimant) unemployment among men in the Rural Development Areas in January 1997 was 16.3%, compared with 15.4% in England as a whole. In the same year, the rate of claimant unemployment in the then Rural Development Areas (RDAs) was 8.1%; whilst that in England as a whole was 9.1% (Beatty *et al*, 1997).[65]
- **Average earnings are lower in rural areas than in urban areas.** Average weekly household earnings in 1999 were £365 in rural districts and £398 in non-rural districts (CACI, 1999). The lowest weekly wages for full-time adult employees at April 1999 were in the predominantly rural counties of Cornwall (£297), Northumberland (£315) and Isle of Wight (£323). The average for England was £405 (ONS, 1999b) (see also Figure 4.6).[66]
- **Rural jobs are more likely than urban jobs to be part-time, casual or seasonal.** In 1999, 26.4% of working people aged 16 and over in rural districts were in part-time employment, compared to 24.7% in England as a whole (ONS, 1999b).
- **Physical isolation in rural areas can make finding and taking up employment difficult** (Breeze *et al*, 2000).

64. 'Hidden unemployment' refers to those of working age who do not have full-time jobs, and are not claiming unemployment-related benefits, but might reasonably be expected to be in work in a fully employed economy. These are found primarily among sickness-benefit claimants (primarily claiming Incapacity Benefit), the prematurely retired, people on government schemes, and people who would like to work but are not eligible to claim benefits (eg. many married women with spouses in work are ineligible to receive income based Jobseekers Allowance) (S Fothergill, personal communication, 2000).

65. Hidden unemployment was estimated by re-working official data.

66. In addition, the self-employed can often be among the lowest earners in rural areas.

Surveys in 1997-98 in four contrasting rural areas and three urban areas[67], revealed that, while the characteristics of the 'detached' male workforce[68] in rural areas were broadly similar to those in urban areas,[69] there were a number of differences[70] (Beatty & Fothergill, 1999) (Figure 4.7). Compared with its urban counterpart, the rural detached male workforce, had:

- higher proportions of older men (ie. over 55), early retirees[71], professional and unskilled workers and people working part-time or in temporary, casual or seasonal work;
- lower proportions with lump-sum redundancy payments or partners in employment;
- proportionally more claiming Housing Benefit and Council-Tax Benefit[72], but fewer claiming under most other benefit categories.
- higher proportions in unpaid or voluntary work (17% of respondents in rural areas engaged in such activities compared with 12% in urban areas).

Figure 4.6 Average annual household earnings per ward, England, 1998

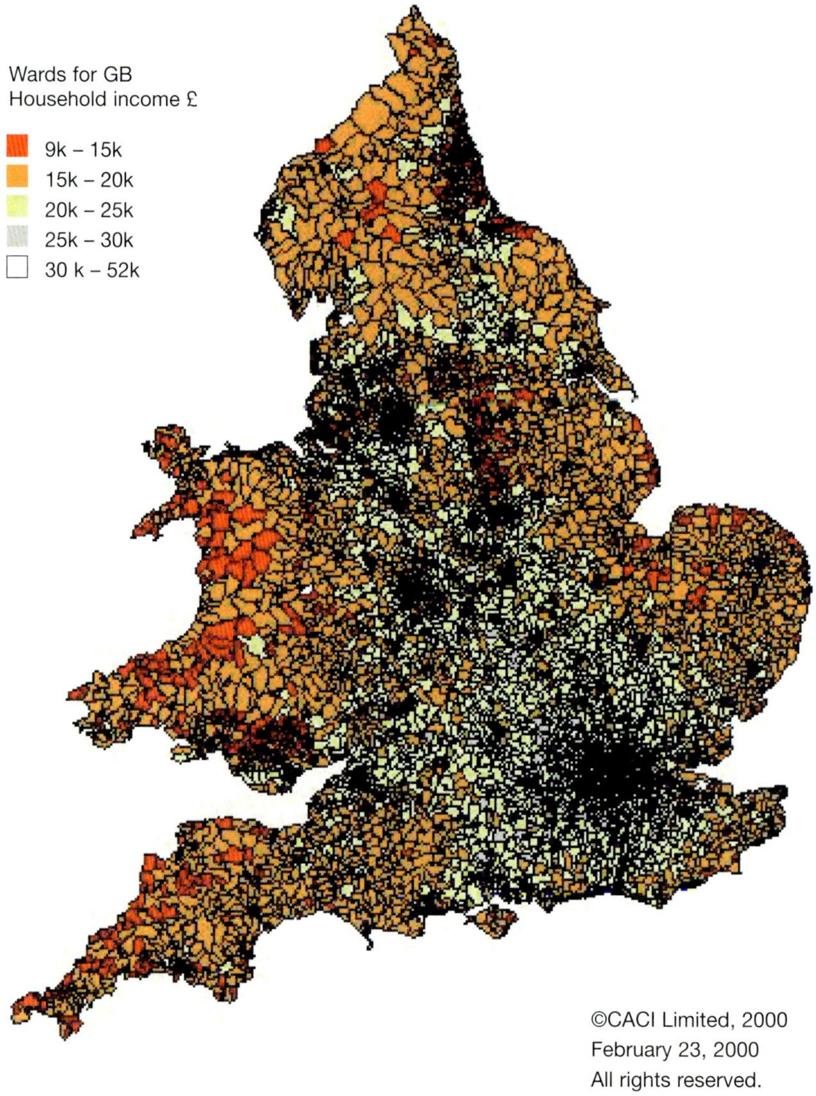

67. Some 500 men in four contrasting rural areas and 1,200 in three urban areas were interviewed using a structured questionnaire between October 1997 and July 1998.

68. Ie. 25–64 year-old men who, at the time of survey, had been unemployed for 6 months or more, were economically active or working only part time.

69. In both cases, the largest groupings were the long-term sick or disabled and the claimant unemployed, the main source of financial support was the benefits system, followed by pensions, and the largest age-group was 55–64 years.

70. The surveys also revealed appreciable differences between rural areas. For example, at one extreme, the depressed local economy of West Cumbria, with a traditional background in industry, had a preponderance of long-term unemployed; by contrast, the villages of upland North Yorkshire, located in a National Park, had a particularly high proportion of early retirees (Beatty & Fothergill, 1999).

71. As many as 30% of these had moved to their present rural area to retire; of all men of working age without full-time jobs, this is probably the least problematic group.

72. This may reflect higher rent levels.

Figure 4.7 Comparison of 25–64 year-old men detached from the labour force in sample rural and urban areas

	Rural sample %	Urban sample %	National estimate %
Self-declared status			
Long-term sick or disabled	32	39	37
Unemployed	25	27	27
Retired	22	16	17
Part-time worker	11	9	10
Full-time carer/looking after home	7	5	5
Other	4	4	4
Age (years)			
25–34	14	16	16
35–44	15	20	20
45–54	21	23	24
55–64	50	41	40
Social class			
Professional	6	3	3
Intermediate	23	16	18
Skilled non-manual	11	14	14
Skilled/semi-skilled manual	40	58	56
Unskilled	20	9	9
Sources of financial support[73]			
Regular paid part-time work	15	12	15
Temporary/casual/seasonal paid work	8	5	6
Pension	36	35	35
Lump-sum redundancy payment	15	21	20
Partner in work	20	26	27
Benefits system	71	75	71

Source: Beatty & Fothergill (1999)

Some obstacles to re-employment are particularly acute in rural areas (Breeze *et al*, 2000; Monk *et al*, 1999):

- **Difficulty getting to work can place a severe constraint on taking up a new job.**[74]
- The relative narrowness of rural economies means **the range of local opportunities is very limited.**
- There are often mismatches between the skills and the jobs available.[75]
- The costs of entering the labour market, for example, of transport or child care, may be prohibitive.[76]

Recent research (Midgley *et al*, 2000) has developed a number of composite indicators (or 'bundles') of employment disadvantage.[77] These suggest that, compared with the more urban wards, a higher proportion of people in the more rural wards may be disadvantaged

73. These headings are not mutually exclusive.

74. Sparsity of employment and physical separation mean, for many, workplaces are some distance from home. Public transport is not usually an option. A survey in 1999 of men without full-time work in four contrasting rural areas revealed a low level of car ownership among those seeking work: only 32% had a car or van in their household that would be available for them to travel to work (Breeze et al, 2000). Even access to employment services can be a problem.

75. Access to colleges to gain additional qualifications can be an additional constraint.

76. Tied housing can also be an obstacle to re-employment. An important source of accommodation in rural areas, tied housing makes changing jobs difficult.

77. These are based, primarily, on 1991 Census data (but drawing also on New Earnings Survey 1998 and the Annual Employment Survey 1997) and enable the proportion of people disadvantaged in a range of ways to be estimated and mapped at ward and district level.

with respect to quality of employment, and in the most rural wards in relation to male low earnings (Figure 4.8).

Figure 4.8 Average proportions of people in each ward in England disadvantaged in accessing employment and by employment quality and low earnings in relation to rurality[78]

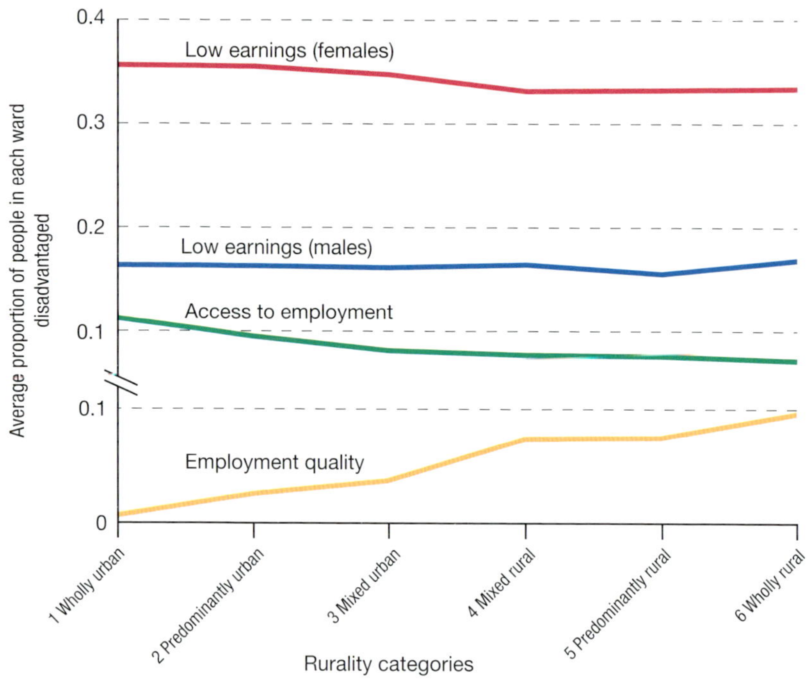

Source: Midgley et al (2000)

New jobs

Some of the changes in rural areas may, in fact, be generating new job opportunities.

An estimated 300,000 full-time equivalent jobs in rural England are attributable to tourism (Geoff Broom Associates, 1998).

A survey of households in 5 contrasting rural areas concluded that **in-migration strengthens the trend in employment from primary production to services, and can generate new jobs** (Findlay *et al*, 1999).

- The self-employed urban-to-rural movers surveyed generated, on average, an estimated 1.7 full-time jobs (often in small professional businesses), plus additional part-time jobs.
- Other migrants (eg. employees, retired) created new labour demands, but these were more likely be in lower-paid and part-time service roles.
- In-migration also increased demand for local rural businesses, notably in the building sector.

78. The rurality categories are based on the ONS urban-rural ward classification (Denham, 1984; Craig, 1987; Wallace et al, 1995) as follows:
1 – wholly urban,
2 – predominantly urban,
3 – mixed urban (more urban than rural),
4 – mixed rural (more rural than urban),
5 – predominantly rural,
6 – wholly rural.
The sum of the numbers of unemployed, on government schemes and excess permanently sick is used as an indicator of 'access' to employment. Employment 'quality' combines low earnings with long hours. Low earnings' is based on numbers of full-time employees earning below £250 per week.

Environmental and related concerns may also be generating employment in rural areas.

- According to the RSPB, **the nature conservation sector provided some 10,000 full-time equivalent jobs in Britain in 1997** (Rayment, 1997).
- An evaluation of the 3,900 farms in the Countryside Stewardship Scheme in 1995 (Harrison-Mayfield *et al*, 1996) estimated that the scheme had generated 220 new jobs in local communities (an average of 0.056 per farm) and increased on-farm labour demand by an average of 0.013 jobs per farm.[79]
- The SAFE Alliance's 1997 study of organic farming showed that an average of one extra full-time, part-time or casual job per farm was created after conversion. About half were for marketing, processing and packaging (Hird, 1997).

A survey of the speciality food and drink sector estimated that in 1999 as many as 37,616 people were employed in these firms in England; 66% of the firms responding to this survey were located in rural areas (DTZ Pieda, 1999).

Rural enterprise

New businesses

Businesses in rural areas made up almost 35% of all VAT-registered enterprises at the end of 1997. **However, there are indications that there are fewer new business start-ups in rural areas compared with England as a whole.**

- In 1997, 76.5% of rural districts had rates of business registration for VAT (often a surrogate for new businesses) below the rates for the Region in which they were located (ONS, 1999b).

Firm size

As with England as a whole, small firms are an important component of the economy of rural areas: 91.4% of all VAT-registered enterprises in the Rural Development Areas in 1997 had fewer than 10 employees (see Figure 4.9).[80]

Figure 4.9 Enterprises in Rural Development Areas by number of employees

Size	Number of Firms	Percentage
1–9 employees	106,210	91.4
10–19 employees	6,430	5.5
20–49 employees	2,470	2.2
50–99 employees	580	0.5
100+ employees	455	0.4
Total	116,150	100.0

Source: Countryside Agency (1999d)

79. An assessment of the Welsh Tir Cymen scheme estimated that 263 jobs had been created through the 718 farm agreements in place at the end of 1995/96, equivalent to 0.37 jobs per farm (ADAS, 1996; CCW, 1996). Pretty (1998) attributed the much greater job generation by Tir Cymen compared with Stewardship to the former's emphasis on whole-farm agreements and a closer partnership between farmers and external authorities.

80. These proportions vary not only between regions, but also between the remote rural areas and market towns. For example in a study of business size in 7 market towns with populations of <15,000 and three towns of >15,000 the proportion of micro-businessess (ie those employing fewer than 10 people) varied from almost 84% in Sherborne, Dorset to 75% in Matlock, Derbyshire to 69% in Melton Mowbray, Leicestershire (DTZ Pieda, 1998).

Areas of least prosperity

The county with the lowest level of Gross Domestic Product (GDP) per head in 1996 was Cornwall, one of the most rural counties of England. There were several other predominantly rural counties among the lowest twelve in GDP terms in England (Figure 4.10).

Figure 4.10 Index of GDP per head for the 12 counties with the lowest GDP, 1996 (UK = 100)[81]

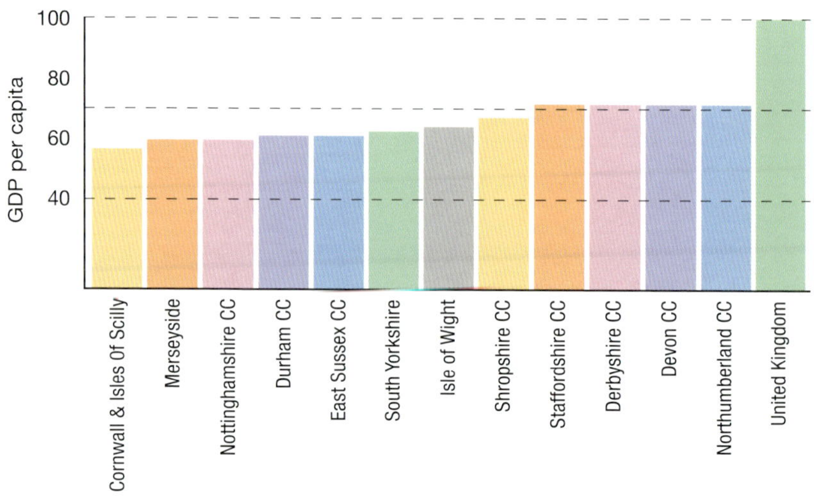

Source: ONS (1999c)

Agriculture

Agriculture is the major land use in England and the main determinant of the appearance and quality of our countryside. The industry has undergone great changes in recent years.

- **Total income from farming and average farm incomes have shown an overall decline in real terms since 1973, as have numbers of farms and farm workers, while average farm size has increased.**
- **Farming's direct contribution to GDP declined through the latter half of the 1990s.**
- **The organic farming sector has grown** in terms both of numbers of producers and demand for organic food. Demand is increasing faster than domestic supply, creating opportunities for further expansion.
- More **farmers are recognising the need to diversify**, in terms both of alternative farm enterprises and off-farm income. For some, successful diversification is likely to be the key to survival.

Key factors impacting on agriculture include: pressures from the World Trade Organisation to reduce support and protection of EU agriculture, together with the wider impacts of globalisation; the enlargement of the EU; the desire by governments to control public expenditure; continuing consumer pressures related to food safety and

81. Data presented for County Councils (CCs) excludes metropolitan unitary authorities.

quality, environment and animal welfare; continuing pressures from supply industries and large retailers, including those arising from a trend towards greater vertical integration (Entec, 2000).

Farming Incomes

Total income from farming (TIFF) has fallen to its lowest level since entering the Common Agricultural Policy. Forecasts for 1999 put the figure at £2.25 billion with income per head at £9,900 (MAFF, 1999a) (Figure 4.11).

- In the Less Favoured Areas (LFAs) of England, where livestock rearing is supported[82] in recognition of its importance to the landscape and local economy, net farm income for all LFA cattle and sheep full-time farms fell from £13,600 in 1997/8 to a forecast of £4,500 in 1999/2000 (MAFF, 1999a).
- The rise in income experienced by most sectors during the mid 1990s was reversed during 1998/99 by depressed prices. The non-milk livestock sectors all reached negative income points in 1998/99, with all other sectors also experiencing sharp declines (MAFF, 1999b) (Figure 4.12).

Figure 4.11 Farm incomes at 1999 prices, UK, 1973–1999

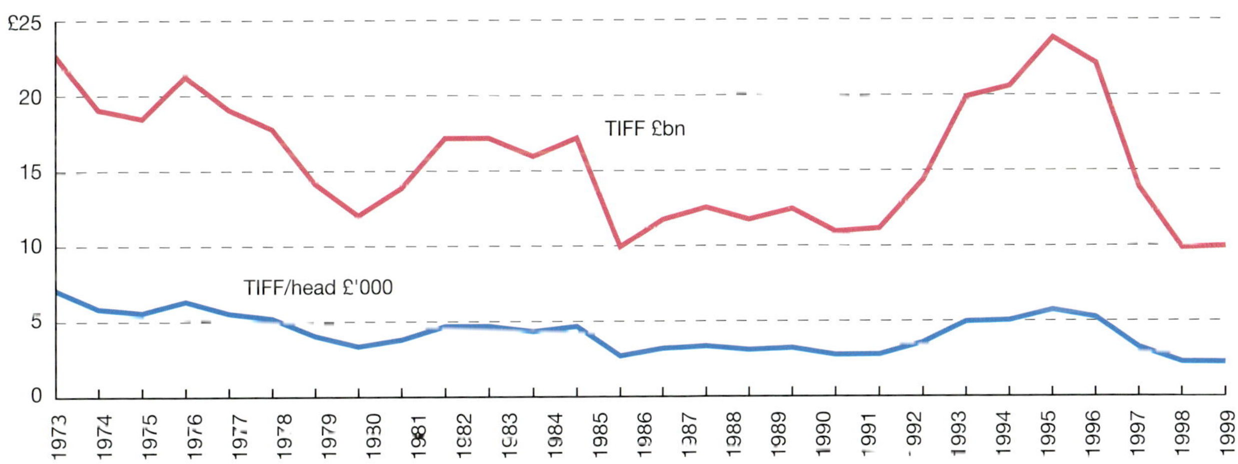

Source: MAFF (1999b)

82. Hill Livestock Compensatory Amounts totalled £114 million in the UK in 1998/99. They are paid over and above the main livestock subsidies.

Figure 4.12 Net farm income by farm type, England, 1990/91–1998/99

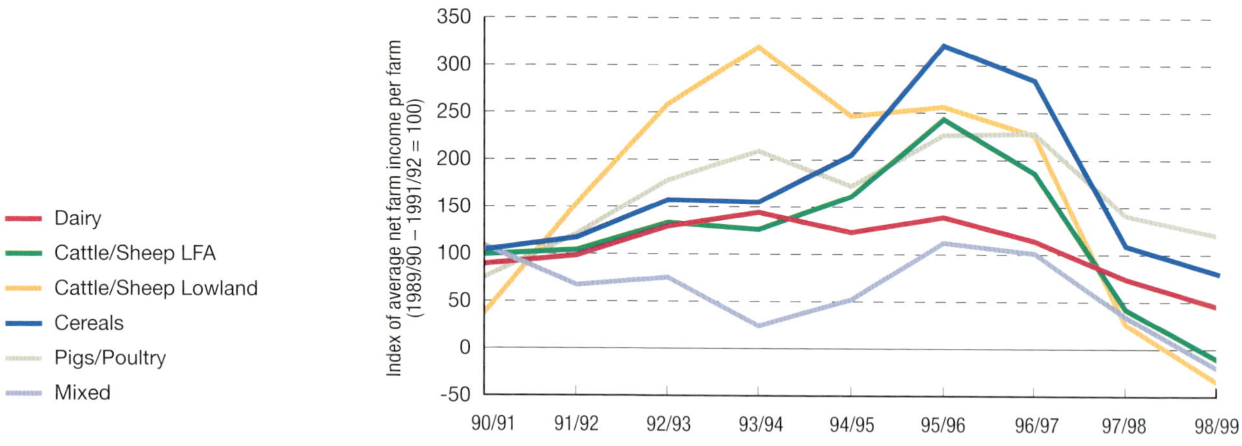

Source: MAFF (1999b)

Employment in agriculture

Employment in agriculture continues its long-term decline.

- The greatest decline has been in regular full-time workers, with higher proportions of part-time labour and also more part-time farmer employment (MAFF, 1999a) (Figures 4.13, 4.14).
- The pattern of agricultural employment varies greatly across the country; in some areas, agriculture is still a major employer (Figure 4.15).

Figure 4.13 Employment in agriculture, England, 1987–1999

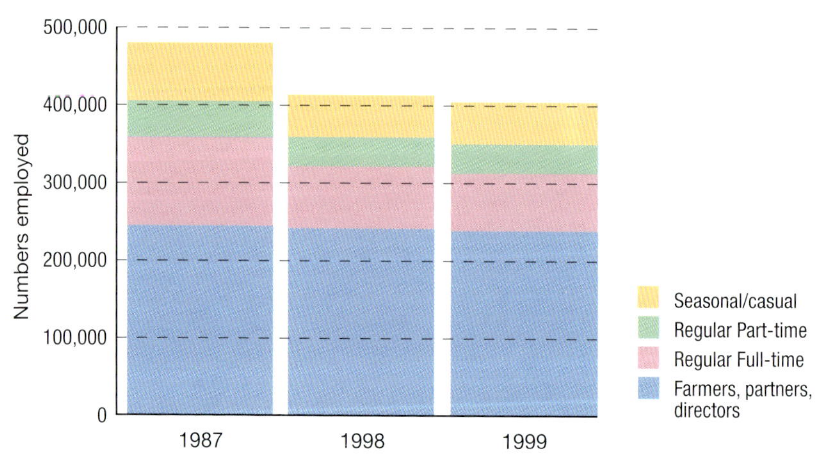

Source: MAFF (1991, 1999a, 1999c)

Figure 4.14 Agricultural employment projections, England, 1985–2005

	1985	1990	1995	2000	2005
Full time	129.5	118.8	110.1	102.0	94.7
Part time	47.3	50.3	55.8	62.5	67.5
Total	176.8	169.1	165.9	164.5	162.2

Source: NFU (1998)

Figure 4.15 Total number of people employed in agriculture by parish, 1998

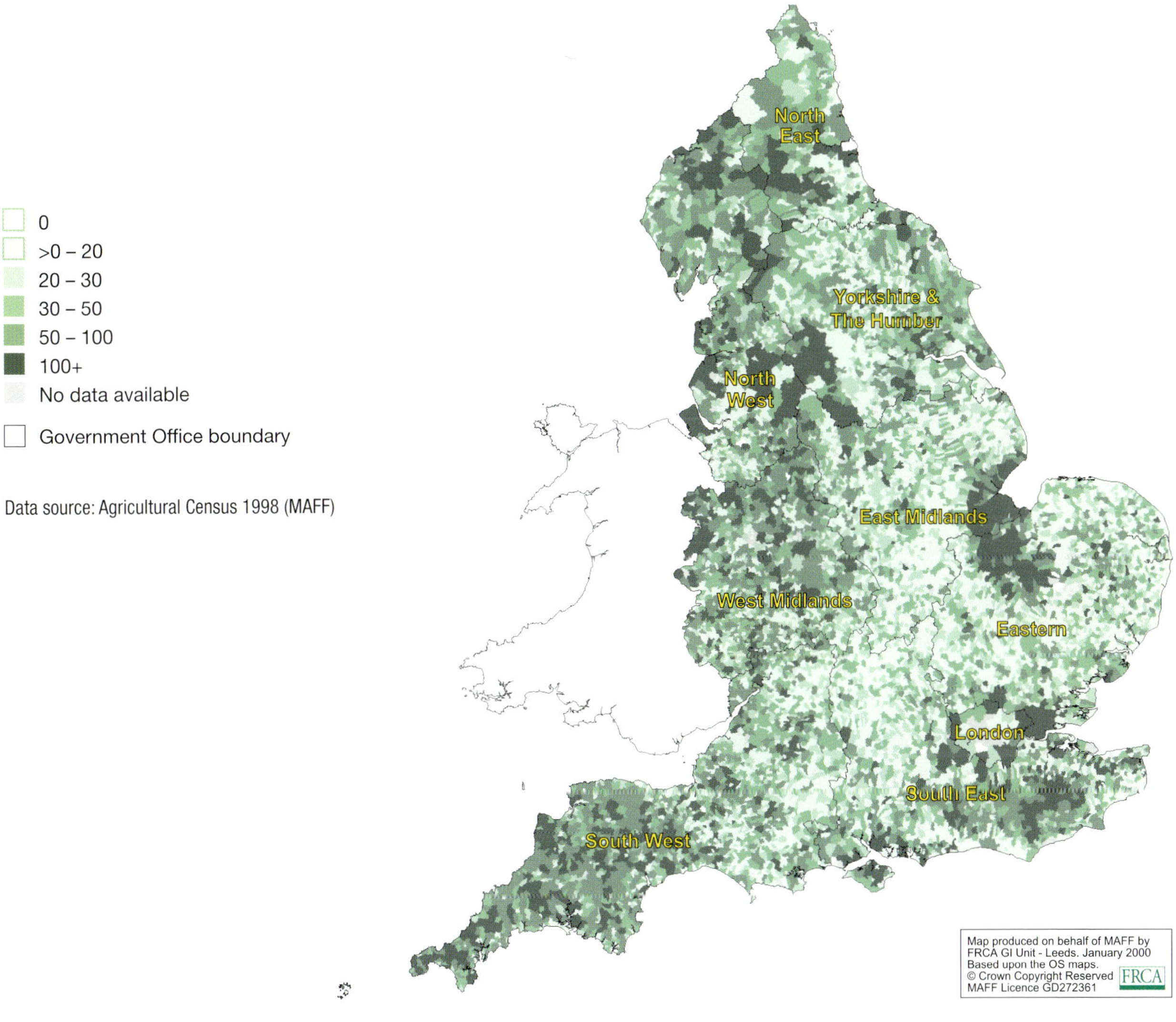

Data source: Agricultural Census 1998 (MAFF)

Land use

There were 9,215,000 hectares of agricultural land (excluding common rough grazing) in England in 1999.

- This was divided into 145,093 holdings (MAFF, 1999a).
- One third was rented (3,148,000 ha) (MAFF, 1999a).

In 1997, 5.3% of holdings were of less 20 ha, 30.4% between 20 and 100 ha, 37.2% between 100 and 300 ha, and 27.2% larger than 300 hectares (MAFF, 1999a).

Agriculture in the national economy

In the latter half of the 1990s, agriculture's contribution to GDP decreased (Figure 4.16). Public expenditure increased between 1994/95 and 1996/97 (mostly due to BSE-related payments) and decreased thereafter (Figures 4.17 and 4.18).

Figure 4.16 Agriculture's contribution to GDP at 1999 prices, UK, 1987–1998

	Av '87–89	1994	1995	1996	1997	1998
£ million	6,506	9,180	10,084	9,782	8,217	7,298
% GDP	1.6	1.6	1.7	1.5	1.2	1

Source: MAFF (1999b)

Figure 4.17 Public expenditure (£ million) on agriculture, UK, 1994/95–1998/99[83]

	1994/95	1995/96	1996/97	1997/98	1998/99 (f)
Total	2,511.5	2,896.8	4,317.7	3,582.8	3,554.8
EC refunds	2,478.2	2,668.3	3,201.2	2,957.8	2,943.2

Source: MAFF (1999b)

Figure 4.18 Public expenditure on agriculture by support measure, UK, 1994/95–1998/99

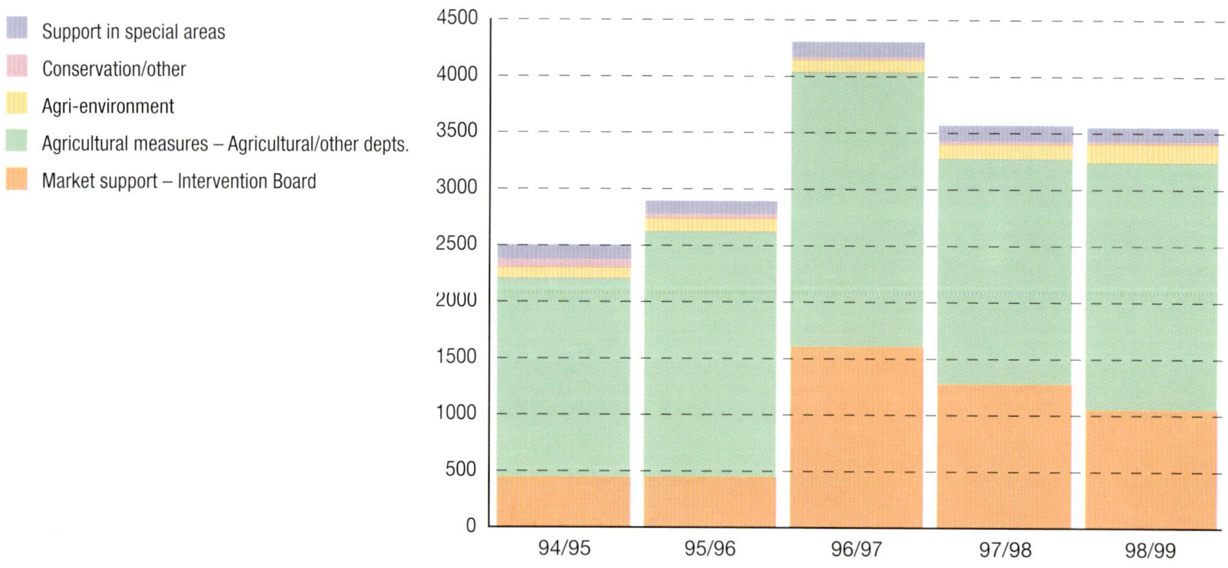

Source: MAFF (1999b)

Expenditure under agri-environmental measures has seen a steady increase from £99 million in 1994/5 to £169 million in 1998/9.

- Of these measures, Countryside Stewardship Scheme increased from £14.9 million to £24 million with 127,753 ha under agreement in England.
- Support under the Organic Aid Scheme increased from £0.3 million in 1995/6 to £2.9 million in 1998/99; the scheme covers 71,520 ha.

83. Government contributions make up the shortfall between total expenditure and funds provided via the EC. Special BSE market support measures accounted for over £1.2 bn. in 1996/7, £0.8 bn. in 1997/8 and £0.4 bn. in 1998/99.

- Although small in terms of total CAP spend, of increasing significance has been the component for agri-environment and rural development measures (encompassed from 1 January 2000 within the Rural Development Regulation) This has increased from £1.1 million in 1995/6 to £7.7 million in 1998/9 (MAFF, 1999b).

Organic farming

The area of land in organic farming has increased and now accounts for some 1.3% of the agricultural area of England.

- 79% of organic land is pasture, with 46% unimproved rough grazing; 135,000 ha are registered, of which, 100,000 ha are in conversion.
- producers increased from 400 in April 1998 to 700 in April 1999, with licensed organic processors numbering 2,101.

Demand for organic food is increasing at 40% per year, supply at only 25% per year. There are, therefore, appreciable opportunities for growth in production.

- Domestic supply satisfies 100% of organic egg demand, 95% of meat, but only 18% for fruit and vegetables.
- The growth in local and organic marketing has seen the number of registered farmers markets rise from 2 in March 1998 to 30 in March 1999, and by the end of 1999 there were over 120 in England[84].
- At present, 45,000 families participate in 'box schemes' worth an estimated £22m, and farm-gate sales generate another £34 million (Soil Association, 1999).

Diversification

Pressures on the agricultural core of farm businesses have led to an exploration of alternative uses for farm resources, including alternative land uses and enterprises, adding value to existing produce through marketing, and farm based non agricultural enterprises. The ADAS Farmers Voice survey found in 1999 that **53% of farmers were considering some form of diversification, with 27% of farmers likely to develop non-farming sources of income**. Although limited in overall employment potential terms, diversification can help to sustain both farming incomes and employment in rural areas. Different opportunities are available both sectorally and regionally with the location of markets a key factor (ADAS, 2000).

Tourism and recreation

Tourism

Tourism is a very important element of rural economies, providing jobs and supporting local services (see Figure 4.19).

84. These figures refer to farmers markets selling locally produced organic produce and/or conventional produce.

- However, employment supported by visitor spending (tourists and leisure day visitors) in the countryside is estimated to have fallen overall by 4% between 1994 and 1998 (with a decline in the accommodation and catering sectors partly offset by growth in the attractions and travel sectors).
- **While total spending by UK tourists in England between 1994 and 1998 increased by 2.4%, spending in the countryside decreased by 3%** (Figure 4.20) across all sectors (Figure 4.20). Countryside spending fell by as much as 20% in some regions, including Yorkshire, East Midlands, Heart of England and the South East.
- **In contrast, spending by overseas visitors on countryside holidays increased by 37% from £509m in 1994 to £699m in 1998** (Figure 4.20), most significantly in the attractions and retailing sectors (Figure 4.21).

Figure 4.19 Changes in employment supported by visitor spending in the countryside 1994–1998.

	1994	1998	Change	% change
Direct jobs	300,877	289,979	-10,898	-4%
Indirect jobs	36,299	33,445	-2,854	-8%
Induced jobs	16,859	16,171	-688	-4%
Total employment	354,035	339,595	-14,440	-4%

Source: Geoff Broom Associates (1998).

Figure 4.20 Gross spending by UK and overseas tourists in England, 1994 and 1998 (£m)

	All spending £m		Estimated spending in the countryside £m		% all spending	
	1994	1998	1994	1998	1994	1998
UK tourists	10,620	10,875	2,130	2,069	20	19
Overseas tourists	8,664	11,204	509	699	6	6

Source: Geoff Broom Associates (1998), ONS (1998), NCSR (1994, 1998).

Figure 4.21 Expenditure in the countryside by UK and overseas tourists by sector, England, 1994 and 1998 (£m)

Sector	Net spend 1994		Net spend 1998	
	UK tourists	Overseas tourists	UK tourists	Overseas tourists
Accommodation	730	188	712	233
Retail	221	123	214	182
Eating & drinking	511	117	506	144
Attractions	116	36	102	76
Travel	441	44	382	64
All	2,019	508	1,916	699

Source: Geoff Broom Associates (1998), ONS (1998), NCSR (1994, 1998).

Day visitors to the countryside

The number of leisure day visits in England as a whole appears to have increased in recent years, although the number of visits to the countryside has slightly declined. Spending on day visits, however, has increased at all locations (Figure 4.22).

- **Between 1996 and 1998, the proportion of total leisure day visits that were visits to the countryside decreased by 3%,** while the proportion to the seaside increased by 16% and to towns and cities by 6%.
- In 1998, the average amount spent on each trip to town/city (£14.00) and seaside trip (£10.40) was much higher than expenditure on trips to the countryside (£6.70). Town/city trips accounted for 84% of total expenditure, countryside 13% and seaside 3%.
- The most popular activities of visitors to the countryside in 1998 were walking (34% of visits), eating/drinking out (14% of visits) and visiting friends or relatives (13% of visits).
- The car was the main mode of transport, accounting for more than half (56%) of all trips; walking was the second most common form of transport (accounting for a further 31% of trips). Fewer than 1% of visits to the countryside were made by public transport.

Figure 4.22 Numbers of leisure day visits and associated expenditure, England, 1996 and 1998

		1996	1998
No. of visits (million)	Total	5,063	5,287
	Countryside	1,302	1,253
Spend per visit	Total	£9.10	£12.10
	Countryside	£5.10	£6.70
Total visitor spend	Total	£45.9bn	£64 bn
	Countryside	£6.7bn	£8 bn

Source: NCSR (1998)

As most visits to the countryside are car based, their decline may be explained in part by the rise in the number of people who see traffic congestion, especially on motorways, as a serious problem, and who may also be deterred by increased fuel prices.

5 Transport that serves people's needs without destroying the environment

Countryside Agency

Windermere, Cumbria.

Transport is a key issue in rural areas, due to both the transport needs associated with the lower densities of population, workplaces and services in rural areas, and to the impacts of transport on the rural environment.

Most rural people rely on their cars for the majority of journeys. Car ownership is higher, on average, and journeys are longer (and take more time) in rural areas than in urban areas; average distances from homes to bus stops and railway stations are greater and public transport less frequent.

Levels of traffic are increasing faster on rural roads than on other roads. While more road accidents occur in towns, they are more likely to be fatal on rural roads. Casualty rates are falling, but this is slowest on minor rural roads. Roads in the countryside are becoming increasingly hazardous for pedestrians, cyclists and riders.

Car ownership and use

The majority of people living in rural England use their cars for most journeys. The location of services and poorer public transport provision compared with urban areas makes car ownership a necessity for most rural households.

- The greater need for a car in rural areas is widely perceived: 93% of people surveyed in the 1999 British Social Attitudes Survey thought 'you are more likely to need a car if you live in the countryside'.
- Some 83% of rural households have a car compared to the national average of 70%. Rural households are twice as likely to run more than one car compared to metropolitan areas (Figure 5.1) (DETR, 1999b).

Figure 5.1 Household car ownership by settlement type, 1996/98

Settlement type	% No car	% 1 car	% 2 cars	% 3 + cars
London & Metropolitan areas	40	42	15	2
Medium to large urban (25K to >250K)	31	47	20	4
Small urban (3K to 25K)	22	46	27	5
Rural (<3K)	17	46	30	7

Source: DETR (1999b)

Rural journeys

Journeys in rural areas are normally longer, more frequent and take more time than urban equivalents (Figure 5.2):

- The average car journey in rural areas is 10 miles, compared to 8 miles for urban car-trips.
- Although journey purposes vary little between urban and rural areas, people in rural areas travel an average 52 miles a week further than people in cities and large towns (DETR, 1999b).

Figure 5.2 Comparison of urban and rural journeys

	Urban	Rural
No of journeys per week	20.1	20.5
Time spent travelling per day	58 minutes	62 minutes
Distance travelled per week	123 miles	175 miles

Source: DETR (1999b)

Public transport

The availability and uptake of public transport remains an issue in rural areas:

- 67.5% of people surveyed in the 1999 British Social Attitudes Survey thought the government should improve public transport in country areas (although this does not necessarily mean that people are willing to switch to using public transport).
- **Less than one third of rural pensioners use the schemes that are available to them** (Figure 5.3) (DETR, 1999b).
- Distances between households and the nearest bus stop have changed little in 10 years. **Overall 89% of households in Great Britain were within 6 minutes walk of a bus stop in 1996/98, but this drops to 77% for rural households** (see Figure 5.4). These figures drop further to 66% for all households and 16% for rural households in Great Britain for bus services operating at frequencies of 30 minutes or less.
- **Few rural households had an easy walk to rail services in 1996/98** (see Figure 5.5) with little change over the preceding 10 years making rail use for long-distance commuting and business travel dependent on modal interchange, either involving bus links, or especially a car journey (DETR, 1999b).

Figure 5.3 Availability and uptake of concessionary fare schemes by area type, 1989/91 to 1996/98

	Pensioners with scheme available (%)			Take up rate (%)		
	1989/91	1992/94	1996/98	1989/91	1992/94	1996/98
London Boroughs	100	100	100	82	83	82
Metropolitan built-up areas	100	100	100	86	83	76
Large urban over 250K	99	100	99	59	58	49
Medium urban over 25K to 250K	95	97	98	56	53	45
Small urban 3K to 25K	89	98	94	41	48	43
Rural	73	91	96	37	45	31
All areas	93	98	98	60	60	52

Source: DETR (1999b)

Figure 5.4 Distribution (% households) of times taken to walk to nearest bus stop by area type, 1985/86 to 1996/98

	Time in minutes 1985/86					Time in minutes 1996/98				
	6 or less	7–13	14–26	27 or more	All households	6 or less	7–13	14–26	27 or more	All households
London Boroughs	86	12	1	–	100	89	9	1	1	100
Metropolitan built-up areas	91	8	1	–	100	92	8	1	–	100
Large urban over 250 K	90	8	2	–	100	90	9	1	–	100
Medium urban over 25K to 250K	90	8	1	–	100	91	7	2	–	100
Small urban 3K to 25K	81	13	3	2	100	82	11	4	2	100
Rural	74	13	7	6	100	77	11	6	6	100
All areas	86	10	2	1	100	87	9	2	1	100

Source: DETR (1999b)

Figure 5.5 Distribution (% households) time taken to walk to nearest rail station by area type, 1985/86 to 1996/98

	Time in minutes 1985/86					Time in minutes 1996/98				
	6 or less	7–13	14–26	27 or more	All households	6 or less	7–13	14–26	27 or more	All households
London Boroughs	27		32	11	100	26	34	31	9	100
Metropolitan built-up areas	8	14	30	48	100	7	10	24	58	100
Large urban over 250K	7	13	26	54	100	7	12	25	56	100
Medium urban over 25K to 250K	5	10	28	57	100	6	12	29	53	100
Small urban 3K to 25K	6	10	18	66	100	4	8	16	71	100
Rural	2	3	7	88	100	3	4	5	88	100
All areas	8	13	24	55	100	8	13	23	57	100

Source: DETR (1999b)

Road safety

Current (1998/99) DETR forecasts estimate that **traffic is rising faster on rural roads than other roads.**

Rural roads are not yet subject to the congestion and localised pollution faced by urban areas, but they are more dangerous. Although incident rates are declining overall, **casualty rates are falling most slowly on minor rural roads and the majority of road deaths are on rural roads** (see Figures 5.6 and 5.7). Some 6% of rural car trips are less than 1 mile (DETR, 1999b). Many of these journeys (eg. to school) are feasible by foot or bike, but the nature of rural roads (eg. absence of footpaths, or a winding hedge-lined route) makes the perceived risk of injury by vehicles too great (CPRE, 1999).

Few off-road bridleways are more than 2 miles long, so many riders have to use sections of public highway on a regular basis. Since April 1st 2000 DETR and rural police authorities have been required to report on accidents involving horses, but official data are not yet available. However, the British Horse Society (personal communication, 1999) reported an estimated 8 per day, totalling some 3,000 every year.

Figure 5.6 Numbers of deaths caused on different road types, 1981–1998

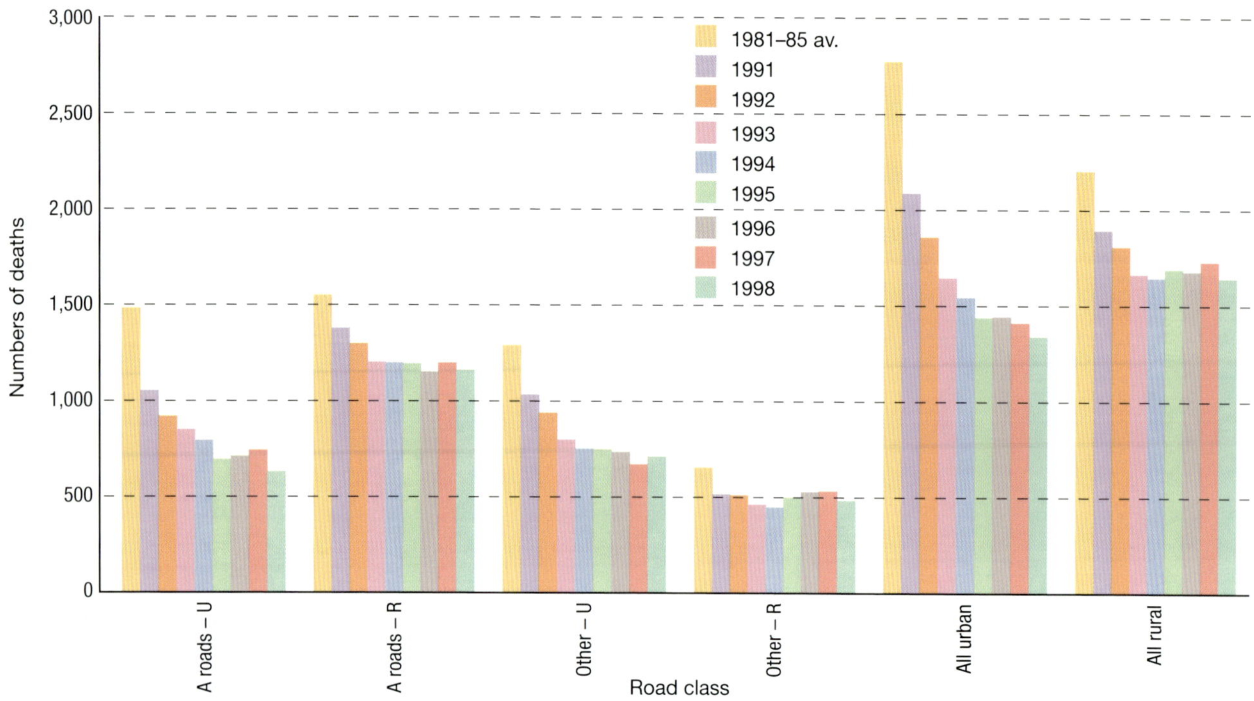

Source: DETR (1999b)

Figure 5.7 Numbers of deaths and serious injuries caused on different road types, 1981–1998

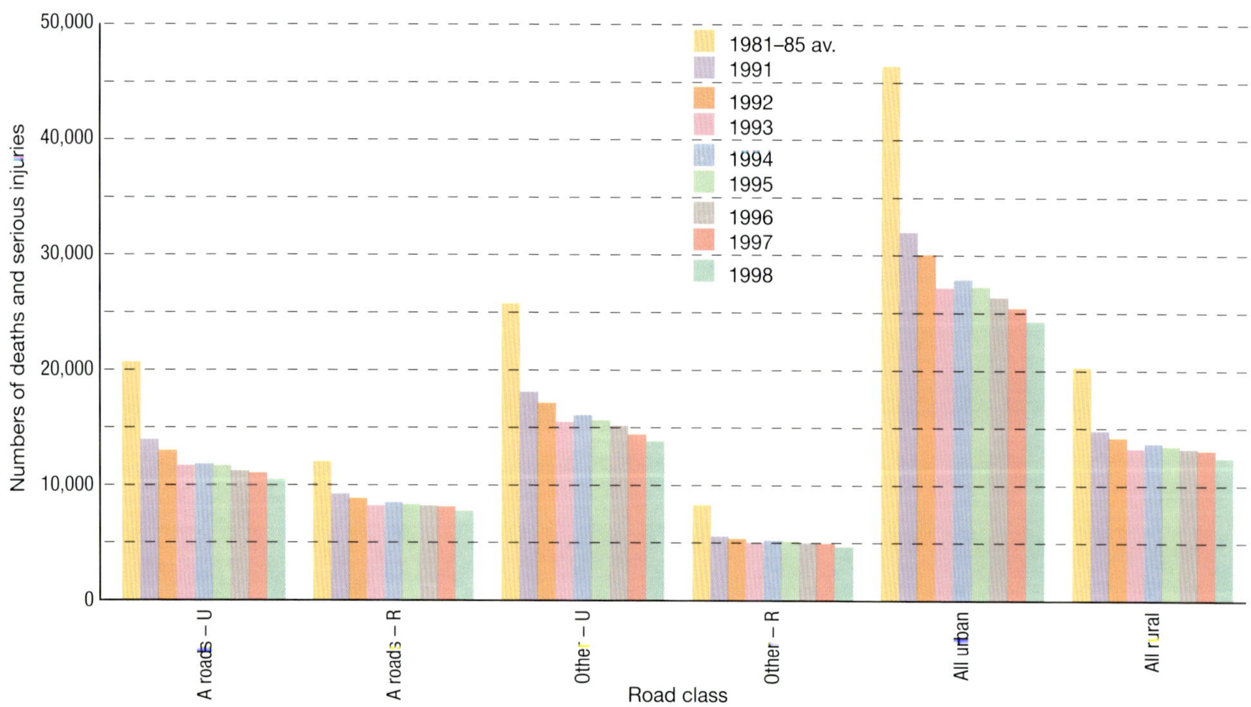

Source: DETR (1999b)

Environmental impacts

Traffic levels are rising faster on rural roads than on other roads (DETR, 1999b). Most new roads in rural areas provide access to new developments or bypass rural settlements. Following the government's strategic review of the trunk-roads network in 1998 the number of proposed rural road schemes dropped from 140 to 37. In 1999, the government switched to considering 'multi-modal' options for 17 study areas which encompass open countryside of local and regional importance, and nationally recognised areas of high landscape value (Figure 5.8). These new schemes aim to find solutions to problems on or with all modes of transport whether they are collections of localised, or apparently isolated, problems (DETR, 1999c). They will consider the impacts of any new infrastructure.

Figure 5.8 Multi-modal studies scheduled by the DETR

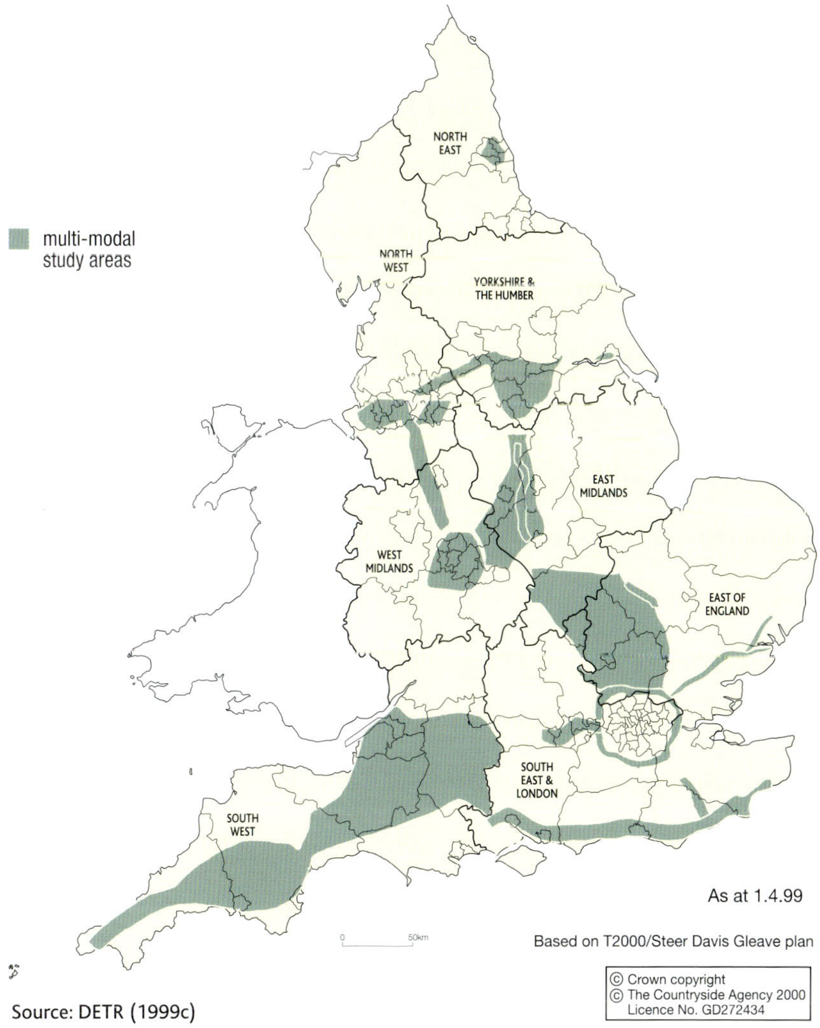

Source: DETR (1999c)

6 Recreational access for local people and visitors

Andy Tryner/Countryside Commission

Brigg, North Lincolnshire.

Being able to walk, ride or cycle in the countryside is essential to enjoying it; and public interest in countryside access and related issues is high. The most important means of access is along some 169,000 km of rights of way. For these to operate effectively they must be legally defined and maintained in good condition. Progress has been made, in recent years, on both fronts, but much remains to be done – both in bringing legal definitions and maps up to date and improving the condition of rights of way. In addition, there is some linear and open access across common land and other land subject to special access agreements. The Government is also committed to legislating, in the 2000/01 Parliamentary session, to create a public right of access on foot over some 1.2–1.8 million ha of open country and registered common land in England and Wales.

Rights of way

England's public rights of way are the single most important means by which the countryside is enjoyed, on foot, horse or bicycle. In some places, they are also important as a means of making local journeys to shops, school and work.

- **The public rights of way network in England comprises an estimated 169,000 km of footpaths, bridleways, Roads Used as Public Paths (RUPPs) and Byways Open to All Traffic (BOATs)** (Figure 6.1).
- Some parts of the network have been designated as 'National Trails'. At present, **there are 10 National Trails open in England together making about 3,000 km of routes** through some of our finest landscapes.[85]
- **The number of local and regional routes has grown considerably in the last 20 years.** These are made up of existing rights of way and may follow routes of high landscape value or historical interest or have some regional or local theme. They are usually described and promoted by parish councils, local community groups, local authorities or national interest organisations.[86]

Figure 6.1 Composition of the public rights of way network in England

Byways	2%	3,000km
RUPPs	3%	5,000km
Bridleways	17%	29,000km
Footpaths	78%	132,000km

Source: Countryside Commission (1996)

In 1987, the then Countryside Commission set a national target for the public rights of way network to be legally defined, properly maintained and well publicised by 2000. This was endorsed by successive governments and by a wide range of other interested bodies.

Local highway authorities have a statutory duty to keep a legal record of all public rights of way in the form of a definitive map and statement. Meeting the target of legal definition involves: bringing the map and statement up to date ('consolidating')[87]; reclassifying RUPPs as byways, bridleways or footpaths, as appropriate; keeping the map and

85. In addition, 3 new National Trails are currently being developed (the Cotswolds Way, Hadrian's Wall Path and the Pennine Bridleway), together extending to some 600 km (see Countryside Agency, 1999e).

86. These routes vary from village or parish paths (eg. the Daffodil Trail and the Poets Way around Dymock, Gloucestershire) to longer-distance routes (eg. the Two Moors Way across Exmoor and Dartmoor in Devon).

87. Ie. To incorporate all diversions, extinguishments and creation orders made since the last map.

statement under continuous review[88]; compiling a rights-of-way record for previously excluded areas[89]. **By 1998, only modest progress had been made towards completing a full legal record of all public rights of way** (Slade, 1999):

- 29% of authorities had consolidated their definitive map;
- 41% of authorities had completed RUPP reclassification;[90]
- there was a backlog of 2,492 applications for modification orders yet to be determined[91], and 9,712 cases, known to highway authorities, that were likely to require a modification order, but were not yet formal applications;[92]
- 34% of authorities had yet to compile a definitive map for previously excluded areas;[93]
- there were 76,850 reported definitive map anomalies requiring rectification.[94]

National surveys of the condition of rights of way network were conducted in 1988 and 1993/94 (Countryside Commission, 1996).[95] These showed that **the condition of rights of way improved in the period from 1988 to 1994 for all users** – walkers, riders and cyclists, although there was still much to be done (Figure 6.2).[96]

- This improvement reflected both growing public interest and awareness and increased activity and expenditure by some local authorities.
- However, it conceals much regional and local variation.

Figure 6.2 Condition of rights of way, England, 1988–1994

	1998 (%)	1994 (%)	Change
1988–1994 (%)			
Paths signposted from the road	34	42	+8
Paths satisfactory to use (free from physical obstruction) by walkers	68	74	+6
Paths properly marked on Ordnance Survey maps	82	88	+6

Source: Countryside Commission (1996)

Access beyond rights of way

At present, there is some linear access beyond rights of way through about 1,900 km^2 of Forestry Commission land and 690 km^2 of land owned by English Nature, and open access across 1,110 km^2 of common land and 480 km^2 of private land through local authority access agreements.

In addition there is linear or open access:

- on some land owned by water companies, the Ministry of Defence and charities such as the National Trust and the Woodland Trust;
- in some private woods receiving access-related management grants from the Forestry Commission;

88. Eg. By confirming a modification order to add a right of way that exists, but has not yet been recorded on the map.

89. Eg. County boroughs which were predominantly urban in character.

90. The total number of RUPPS that had been reclassified was 4,166; 3,305 had yet to be reclassified.

91. There has been an annual increase in the backlog of applications since 1983. The greatest number of applications yet to be determined is within the shire counties. Only 45% of authorities predict that they will have cleared their backlog of modification orders by 2010, under current procedures.

92. It has been estimated that if all of these potential modification orders were confirmed, this would create another 6,382 km of rights of way, a 4% increase to the current total length of the network.

93. Predicted dates for completing this task ranged from 1999–2014.

94. Anomalies occur where the path recorded on the definitive map is not available for public use on the ground. This could be the result of a mistake on the map (eg. if the line was drawn on the wrong side of the hedge or if a path has been built over by development without proper diversion or extinguishment orders being made).

95. The next one is due to take place in 2001.

96. The government is committed to legislating to improve the management of the rights of way network to meet the modern-day requirements of users and land managers.

- on areas of open country with access traditions that are not secured in law (*de facto* access);
- through some areas covered by Countryside Stewardship Schemes;
- through some areas under agreements arising from conditional exemption from capital taxes.

Access to open countryside

The Government is committed to legislating in the 2000/01 Parliamentary session to create a public right of access on foot over 1.2–1.8 million ha of open country (ie. mountain, moor, heath, and down) and registered common land in England and Wales. This access will be subject to restrictions where essential in the interests of nature conservation, heritage, health and safety and land management.

Attitudes to countryside access

Public use of the countryside for recreation and interest in countryside access, and the issues surrounding it, has increased appreciably in recent years.

Of the 899 people questioned in the 1998 British Social Attitudes Survey (Christie & Jarvis, 1999):

- 50% thought a farmer or landowner 'probably' or 'definitely' *should not have the right* to close a rarely-used footpath running through farmland;
- 61% thought a farmer or landowner 'probably' or 'definitely' *should not have the right* to close a rarely-used footpath running through *woodland*;[97]
- 56%, however, thought the new owner of a large estate in a beautiful part of Britain *should have the right* to fence off a remote part of his land to stop people visiting it.

Analysis of the 1998 survey indicated a clear association between support for access to the countryside and overall concern for the environment.

Of the people questioned in the 1999 British Social Attitudes Survey, only 13% agreed that 'the beauty of the countryside depends on stopping too many people from visiting it', 43% agreed that 'some parts of the countryside are now so popular that it's no longer a pleasure to visit them'.

97. In this case, those living in rural areas (71%) are more likely to oppose the farmer's right to close the path than those living in cities, towns or suburbs (58%).

References

ACRE. 1993. *Enabling rural social housing.* A report on the ACRE housing pilot project. Cirencester: Action for Communities in Rural England.

ADAS. 1996. *Socio-economic assessment of Tir Cymen.* Report to the Countryside Council for Wales, Bangor.

ADAS. 2000. *English Agriculture: opportunities for change. Diversification.* Report to the Countryside Agency. Wolverhampton: ADAS.

Anderson, S. 1999. Crime and social change in rural areas. In: *Rural Audit.* London: The Rural Group of Labour MPs.

Barr, C J; Bunce, R G H; Clarke, R T; Fuller, R M; Furse, M J; Gillespie, M K; Croom, G B; Hallam, C J; Hornung, M; Howard, D C & Ness, M J. 1993. *Countryside Survey 1990. Main report.* Countryside 1990 Series, Volume 2. London: Department of the Environment.

Beaton, L. 1998. *Village halls in England 1998.* Cirencester: Action for Communities in Rural England.

Beatty, C & Fothergill, S. 1999. *Labour market detachment among men in rural England.* London: Rural Development Commission.

Beatty, C; Fothergill, S; Gore, T & Herrington, A. 1997. *The local incidence of unemployment in rural development areas.* Report to Rural Development Commission. Sheffield: Centre for Regional and Social Research, Sheffield Hallam University.

Bradley, A. 1987. Poverty and dependency in village England. In: Lowe, P; Bradley, A & Wright (Eds). *Disadvantage and welfare in rural areas.* Norwich: Geo Books.

Bramley, G. 1995. *Rural incomes and housing affordability.* London: Rural Development Commission.

Breeze, J; Fothergill, S & MacMillan, R. 2000. *Matching New Deal to rural needs.* Report to the Countryside Agency. Sheffield: Centre for Regional and Social Research, Sheffield Hallam University.

Brierley, P. 2000. *The tide is running out. What the English Church Attendance Survey reveals.* London: Christian Research.

Brierley, P (Ed). 1999. *UK Christian Handbook. Religious Trends, 2000/20001 No 2.* London: Christian Research & Harper Collins.

CACI. 1999. *CACI data datalogue.* London: CACI

CCW. 1996. *Tir Cymen: 4 years of achivement.* Bangor: Countryside Council of Wales.

Chapman, P; Phiminster, E; Shucksmith, M; Upward, R & Vera-Toscano, E. 1998. *Poverty and social exclusion in rural Britain: the dynamics of low income and employment.* York: York Publishing Services.

Christie, I & Jarvis, L. 1999. Rural spaces and urban jams. In: Jowell, R; Curtice, J; Park, A; Thomson, K; Jarvis, L; Bromley, C & Stratford, N (Eds). *British social attitudes: the 16th report. Who shares New Labour values?* Aldershot: Ashgate.

Clifford, S. 1997. Barefoot through the learning locality. In: *Participation Works.* London: Centre for Community Visions, New Economics Foundation.

Cloke, P; Milbourne, P & Thomas, C. 1994. *Lifestyles in rural England.* London: Rural Development Commission.

Cloke, P; Goodwin, M; Milbourne, P & Thomas, C. 1995. Deprivation, poverty and marginalisation in rural lifestyles in England and Wales. *Journal of Rural Studies* **11** (4), 351–365.

Cloke, P; Milbourne, P; Widdowfield, R. 2000. Homelessness in rural England. In: Cloke, P; Milbourne, P; Widdowfield R (Eds). *Homelessness in rural areas: issues, experiences and policy responses.* Cardiff: Cardiff University.

Countryside Agency. 1999a. *Countryside Character. Volumes 1–8.* CCP 535, CCP 536, CCP 537, CA 10, CA 11, CA 12, CA 13 and CA 14. Cheltenham: Countryside Agency.

Countryside Agency. 1999b. *Regeneration around cities: the role of England's community forests.* CAX 33. Cheltenham: Countryside Agency.

Countryside Agency. 1999c. *Rural services and social housing 1997–1998.* CAX 17. Cheltenham: Countryside Agency.

Countryside Agency. 1999d. *State of the Countryside 1999.* Cheltenham: Countryside Agency.

Countryside Agency. 1999e. *National Trails. An introduction.* CA 15. Cheltenham: Countryside Agency.

Countryside Commission. 1996. *Findings of the national rights of way conditions survey.* Cheltenham: Countryside Commission.

CPRE. 1999. *Rural traffic fear survey,* 1999. London: Council for the Protection of Rural England.

Craig, J. 1987. An urban-rural categorisation for wards and local authorities. *Population Trends* **47**, 6–11.

Cronk, Q C B & Fuller, J L. 1995. *Plant invaders: the threat to natural ecosystems.* People and plants conservation manual. Volume 2. London: Chapman and Hall.

Darvill, T & Fulton, A. 1998. *The monuments at risk survey of England 1995. Main report.* Bournemouth & London:

Bournemouth University & English Heritage.

Denham, C. 1984. Urban Britain. *Population Trends* **36**, 10–18.

Derounian, J. 1993. *Another country. Real life beyond the Rose Cottage*. London: National Council for Voluntary Organisations

DETR. 1998a. *English house condition survey 1996*. London: The Stationery Office.

DETR. 1998b. *Planning and affordable housing*. Circular 06/98. London: Department of the Environment, Transport and the Regions.

DETR. 1998c. *1998 Index of Local Deprivation. A summary of results, 11 June 1998*. London: Department of the Environment, Transport and the Regions.

DETR. 1999a. *Quality of life counts. Indicators for a strategy for sustainable development for the United Kingdom: a baseline assessment*. London: Department of the Environment, Transport and the Regions.

DETR. 1999b. *Transport statistics bulletin. National travel survey. 1996–98 update*. London: Department of the Environment, Transport and the Regions.

DETR. 1999c. *Guidance on the methodology for multi-modal studies*. London: Department of Environment, Transport and the Regions.

DTZ Pieda. 1998. *The nature of demand for housing in rural areas*. London: Department of the Environment, Transport and the Regions.

DTZ Pieda. 1999. *UK speciality food and drink sector. Report to Food From Britain and MAFF*. Edinburgh: DTZ Pieda.

Edwards, A C & Withers, P J A. 1998. Soil phosphorus management water quality: a UK perspective. *Soil Use and Management* **14**, 124–130.

English Nature & Countryside Commission. 1996. *Character of England: landscape, wildlife and natural features*. Cheltenham & Peterborough: Countryside Commission & English Nature.

English Nature. 1999. *Eighth annual report 1998/99*. Peterborough: English Nature.

Entec. 2000. *English agriculture: opportunities for change. Current state and drivers of change*. Report to the Countryside Agency. Leamington Spa: Entec.

Environment Agency. 1996. *Guidance for the control of invasive plants near watercourses*. Bristol: Environment Agency.

Environment Agency. 2000. *The state of the environment of England and Wales*. London: The Stationery Office.

Environment Agency & Scottish Environmental Protection Agency. 1998. *River habitat quality: the physical character of rivers and streams in the UK and Isle of Man*. Bristol & Stirling: Environment Agency & Scottish Environmental Protection Agency.

Findlay, A; Short, D; Stockdale, A. 1999. *Migration impacts in rural England*. CAX 19. Cheltenham: Countryside Agency.

Francis, L J. 1996. *Churchwatch*. London: The Society for Promoting Christian Knowledge.

Geoff Broom Associates. 1998. *The economic impact of recreation and tourism in the English countryside 1998*. London: Rural Development Commission & Countryside Commission.

Gomm, M. 1997. *Housing Strategy*. Cirencester: Housing and Health Department, Cotswold District Council.

Harrison-Mayfield, L; Dwyer, J & Brooks, G. 1996. *The socio-economic effects of the Countryside Stewardship Scheme*. London: Countryside Commission.

Hawton, K; Simkin, S; Malmberg, A; Fagg, J & Harris, L. 1998. *Suicide and stress in farmers*. London: The Stationery Office.

Hedges, A. 1999. *Living in the countryside: the needs and aspirations of rural populations*. Report to the Countryside Agency. Leighton Buzzard: Alan Hedges.

Hird, V. 1997. *Double yield: jobs and sustainable food production*. London: SAFE Alliance.

Housing Corporation. 1999. *National Investment Strategy 2000/2001*. London: Housing Corporation.

Jones, K. 2000. A countryside crisis? In: Harrop, A (Ed). *Changing views of rural Britain*. London: New Policy Institute.

JRF (1999) *Findings. Housing and employment problems for young people in the countryside*. York: Joseph Rowntree Foundation.

Kelly, J. 1997. Community audit in North Kesteven. In: Participation Works. London: Centre for Community Visions, New Economics Foundation.

King, D G. 2000. *Projected household numbers for rural districts of England, 1996–2016*. Report to the Countryside Agency. Chelmsford: The Household Projection Service, Anglia University.

MAFF. 1991. *The digest of agricultural census statistics UK, 1990*. London: The Stationery Office.

MAFF. 1999a. Stats 61/99. *Joint announcement by the agricultural departments of the United Kingdom, 29th November 1999*. London: Ministry of Agriculture, Fisheries and Food.

MAFF. 1999b. *Agriculture in the United Kingdom 1998*. London: The Stationery Office.

MAFF. 1999c. *The digest of agricultural census statistics UK, 1998*. London: The Stationery Office

Massingham, H. J. 1939. *A Countryman's Journal*. London: Chapman & Hall.

Midgley, J; Hodge, I & Monk, S. 2000. *Developing indicators of rural disadvantage. Stage 2*. Report to the Countryside Agency. Cambridge: University of Cambridge.

Mirlees-Black, C. 1998. *Rural areas and crime: findings from the British crime survey*. Research Findings No 77. London: Home Office Research and Statistics Directorate.

Monk, A S. 1999. *Rural isolation as a stressor: physical, cultural, social and psychological isolation in rural areas of Great Britain, Northern Ireland and Eire*. Newport, Shropshire & Stoneleigh, Warwickshire: Countryside Development Unit, Harper Adams University College & Rural Stress Information Network.

Monk, S; Dunn, J; Fitzgerald, M & Hodge, I. 1999. *Finding work in rural areas*. York: Joseph Rowntree Foundation.

Moseley, M; Derounian, J G & Allies, P J. 1996. Parish appraisals – a spur to local action. *Town Planning Review* **67** (3).

Moseley, M. 1997. Parish appraisals as as tool of rural community development: an assessment of the British experience. *Planning practice and Research* **12** (3).

NCSR. 1998. *UK Day Visits Survey, 1998*. London: National Centre for Social Research.

NCSR. 1994. *UK Day Visits Survey, 1994*. London: National Centre for Social Research

NFU. 1998. *Farming Economy 1998*. London: National Farmers Union.

NFU. 1999. *The human cost of the farm crisis. Audit for action*. London: National Farmers Union.

NFU. 2000. *Tenant farms – the facts*. London: National Farmers Union.

ONS. 1998. *International Passenger Survey, 1998*. London: Office for National Statistics.

ONS. 1999a. *Social Trends, 1999*. London: The Stationery Office.

ONS. 1999b. *New earnings survey, 1999*. London: Office for National Statistics.

ONS. 1999c. *Regional Trends, 1999*. London: The Stationery Office.

Palmer, G. 2000. Introduction. In: Harrop, A (Ed). *Changing views of rural Britain*. London: New Policy Institute.

Pretty, J. 1998. *The Living Land*. Earthscan, London

Rayment, M. 1997. *Working with nature in Britain. Case studies of nature conservation, employment and local economies*. Sandy, Bedfordshire: RSPB and Birdlife International.

RDC. 1993. *Homelessness in rural England – statistical update to 1992/93*. Research Report No. 17. London: Rural Development Commission.

RDC. 1995. *Rural incomes and housing affordability*. London: Rural Development Commission.

RDC. 1996. *Rural needs in local authority housing strategies*. London: Rural Development Commission.

RDC. 1997. *Survey of rural services*. London: Rural Development Commission.

RDC. 1998. *Household growth in rural areas*. London: Rural Development Commission.

RDC & Housing Corporation. 1997. *Rural Settlement Gazetteer*. London: Rural Development Commission & Housing Corporation.

SERRL. 2000. *Spatial analysis of rural settlements and services*. Report to the Countryside Agency. London: South East Regional Research Laboratory, Birkbeck College.

Shucksmith, M. 1999. Poverty and social exclusion in rural Britain. In: *Rural Audit*. London: The Rural Group of Labour MPs.

Slade. 1999. *An evaluation of the process of recording public rights of way in England: a report for the County Surveyors Society countryside working group*. Lincolnshire: County Surveyors Society.

Soil Association. 1999. *The organic food and farming report, 1999*. Bristol: Soil Association.

SSLRC. 2000. *Agriculurally accelerated soil erosion by water*. Report to the Countryside Agency. Silsoe: Soil Survey and Land Research Centre.

TCPA. 1999. *The people: where will they work?* Report of TCPA research into the changing geography of employment. London: Department of the Environment, Transport and the Regions.

W S Atkins. 1998. *Design in the countryside: monitoring countryside design summaries and village design statements*. Report to the Countryside Commission. Cambridge: W S Atkins.

Wallace, M; Charlby, J; Denham, C. 1995. The new OPCS area classifications. *Population Trends* **79**, 15–29.

Winter, M; Milbourne, P & Mitra, B. 1999. *Complementarities and conflicts between farming and incomers to the countryside in England and Wales*. Interim progress report to MAFF. Contract RE 0108. Cheltenham: Cheltenham & Gloucester College of Higher Education.

Maps

Rural local authority districts and unitary authorities

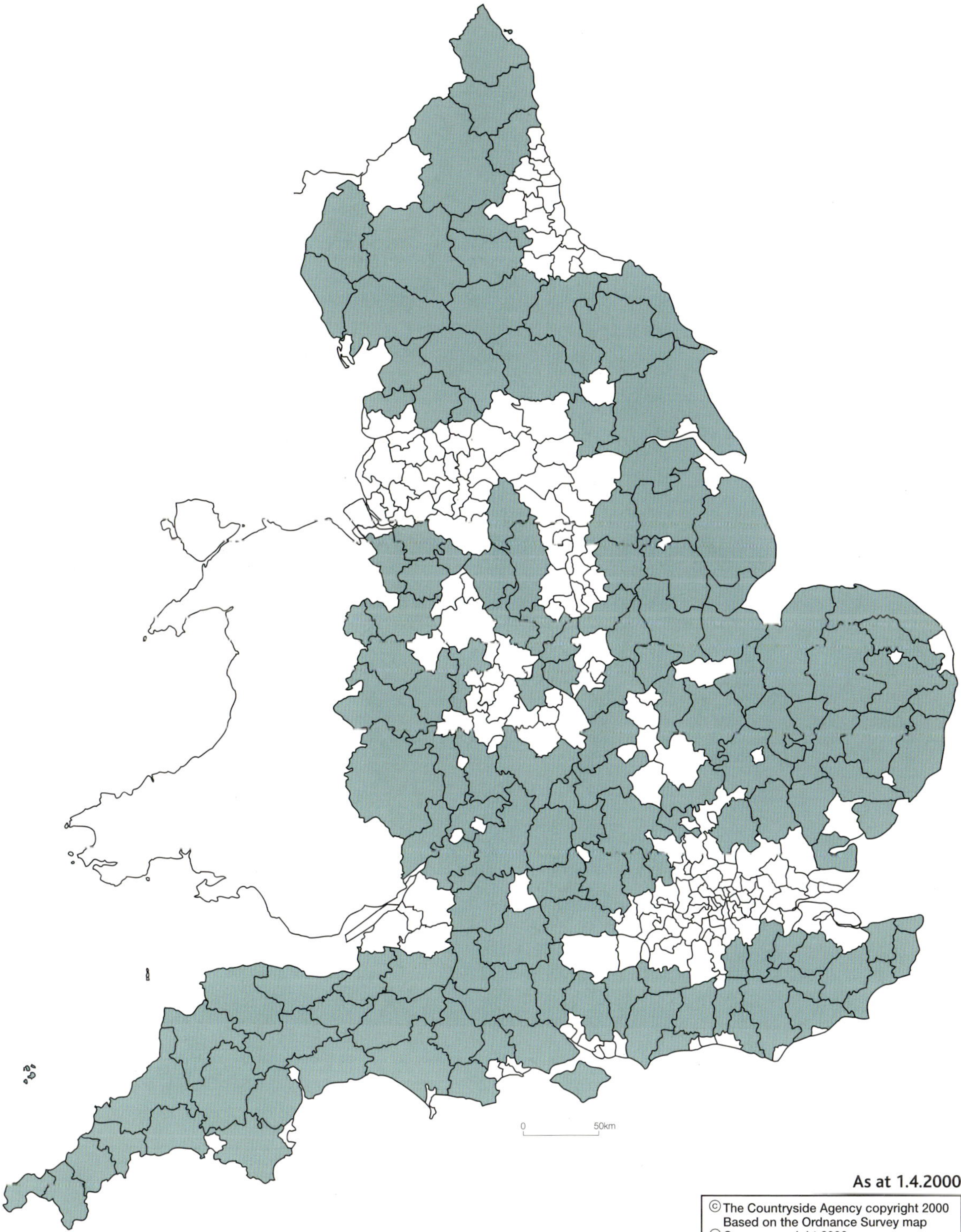

As at 1.4.2000

The character of England: landscape, wildlife and natural features.

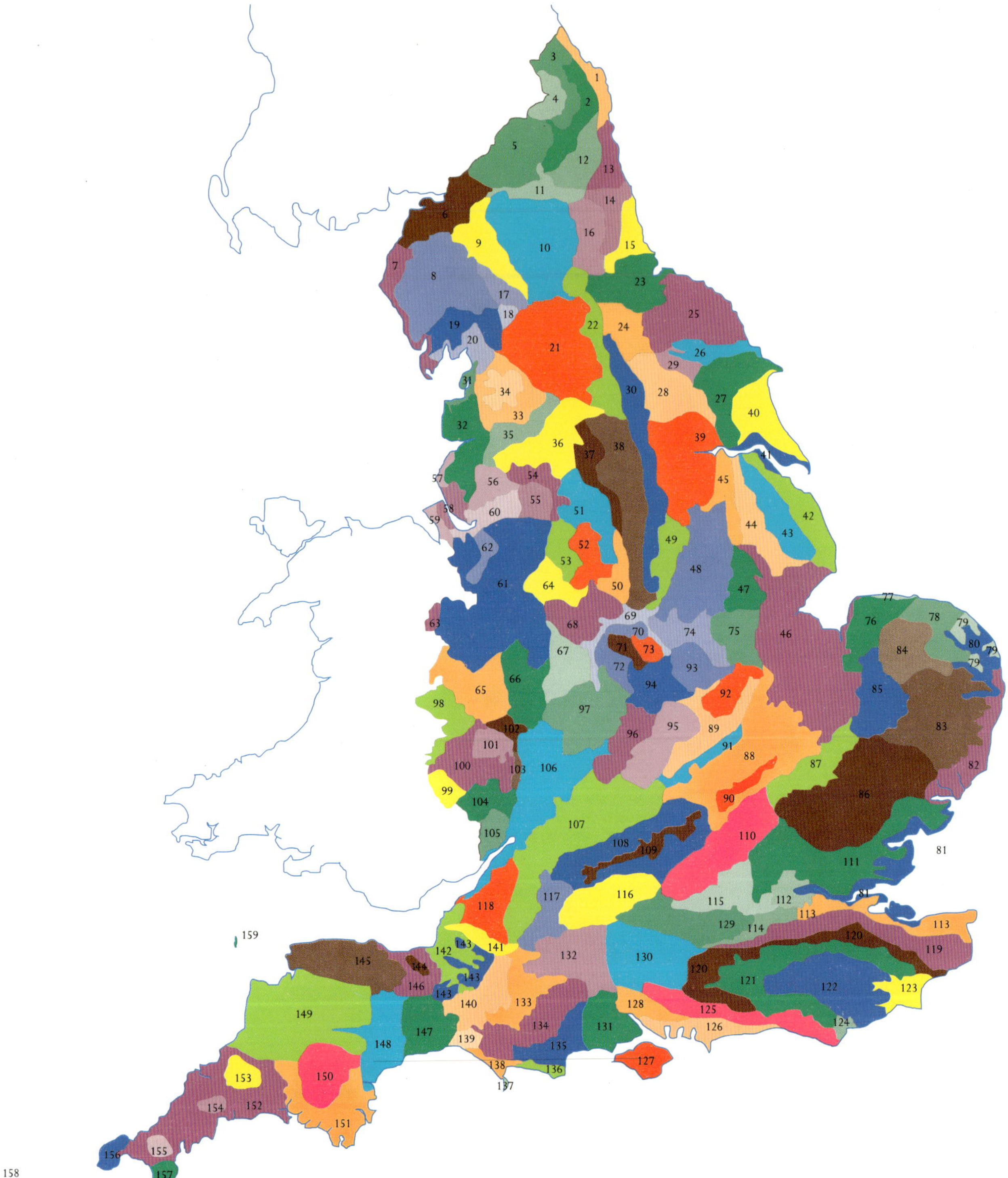

Based on the joint map produced by the Countryside Agency and English Nature, 1996

1 North Northumberland Coastal Plain
2 Northumberland Sandstone Hills
3 Cheviot Fringe
4 Cheviots
5 Border Moors and Forests
6 Solway Basin
7 West Cumbria Coastal Plain
8 Cumbria High Fells
9 Eden Valley
10 North Pennines
11 Tyne Gap and Hadrian,s Wall
12 Mid Northumberland
13 South East Northumberland Coastal Plain
14 Tyne and Wear Lowlands
15 Durham Magnesian Limestone Plateau
16 Durham Coalfield Pennine Fringe
17 Orton Fells
18 Howgill Fells
19 South Cumbria Low Fells
20 Morecambe Bay Limestones
21 Yorkshire Dales
22 Pennine Dales Fringe
23 Tees Lowlands
24 Vale of Mowbray
25 North Yorkshire Moors and Cleveland Hills
26 Vale of Pickering
27 Yorkshire Wolds
28 Vale of York
29 Howardian Hills
30 Southern Magnesian Limestone
31 Morecambe Bay and Lune Estuary
32 Lancashire and Amounderness Plain
33 Bowland Fringe and Pendle Hill
34 Bowland Fells
35 Lancashire Valleys
36 Southern Pennines
37 Yorkshire Southern Pennine Fringe
38 Nottinghamshire, Derbyshire and Yorkshire Coalfield
39 Humberhead Levels
40 Holderness
41 Humber Estuary
42 Lincolnshire Coast and Marshes
43 Lincolnshire Wolds
44 Central Lincolnshire Vale
45 Northern Lincolnshire Edge with Coversands
46 The Fens
47 Southern Lincolnshire Edge
48 Trent and Belvoir Vales
49 Sherwood
50 Derbyshire Peak Fringe
51 Dark Peak
52 White Peak
53 South West Peak
54 Manchester Pennine Fringe
55 Manchester Conurbation
56 Lancashire Coal Measures
57 Sefton Coast
58 Merseyside Conurbation
59 Wirral
60 Mersey Valley
61 Shropshire, Cheshire and Staffordshire Plain
62 Cheshire Sandstone Ridge
63 Oswestry Uplands
64 Potteries and Churnet Valley
65 Shropshire Hills
66 Mid Severn Sandstone Plateau
67 Cannock Chase and Cank Wood
68 Needwood and South Derbyshire Claylands
69 Trent Valley Washlands
70 Melbourne Parklands
71 Leicestershire and South Derbyshire Coalfield
72 Mease/Sence Lowlands
73 Charnwood
74 Leicestershire and Nottinghamshire Wolds
75 Kesteven Uplands
76 North West Norfolk
77 North Norfolk Coast
78 Central North Norfolk
79 North East Norfolk and Flegg
80 The Broads
81 Greater Thames Estuary
82 Suffolk Coast and Heaths
83 South Norfolk and High Suffolk Claylands
84 Mid Norfolk
85 Breckland
86 South Suffolk and North Essex Clayland
87 East Anglian Chalk
88 Bedfordshire and Cambridgeshire Claylands
89 Northamptonshire Vales
90 Bedfordshire Greensand Ridge
91 Yardley-Whittlewood Ridge
92 Rockingham Forest
93 High Leicestershire
94 Leicestershire Vales
95 Northamptonshire Uplands
96 Dunsmore and Feldon
97 Arden
98 Clun and North West Herefordshire Hills
99 Black Mountains and Golden Valley
100 Herefordshire Lowlands
101 Herefordshire Plateau
102 Teme Valley
103 Malvern Hills
104 South Herefordshire and Over Severn
105 Forest of Dean and Lower Wye
106 Severn and Avon Vales
107 Cotswolds
108 Upper Thames Clay Vales
109 Midvale Ridge
110 Chilterns
111 Northern Thames Basin
112 Inner London
113 North Kent Plain
114 Thames Basin Lowlands
115 Thames Valley
116 Berkshire and Marlborough Downs
117 Avon Vales
118 Bristol, Avon Valleys and Ridges
119 North Downs
120 Wealden Greensand
121 Low Weald
122 High Weald
123 Romney Marshes
124 Pevensey Levels
125 South Downs
126 South Coast Plain
127 Isle Of Wight
128 South Hampshire Lowlands
129 Thames Basin Heaths
130 Hampshire Downs
131 New Forest
132 Salisbury Plain and West Wiltshire Downs
133 Blackmoor Vale and Vale of Wardour
134 Dorset Downs and Cranborne Chase
135 Dorset Heaths
136 South Purbeck
137 Isle of Portland
138 Weymouth Lowlands
139 Marshwood and Powerstock Vales
140 Yeovil Scarplands
141 Mendip Hills
142 Somerset Levels and Moors
143 Mid Somerset Hills
144 Quantock Hills
145 Exmoor
146 Vale of Taunton and Quantock Fringes
147 Blackdowns
148 Devon Redlands
149 The Culm
150 Dartmoor
151 South Devon
152 Cornish Killas
153 Bodmin Moor
154 Hensbarrow
155 Carnmenellis
156 West Penwith
157 The Lizard
158 Isles of Scilly
159 Lundy

The Countryside Agency's designated and defined interests

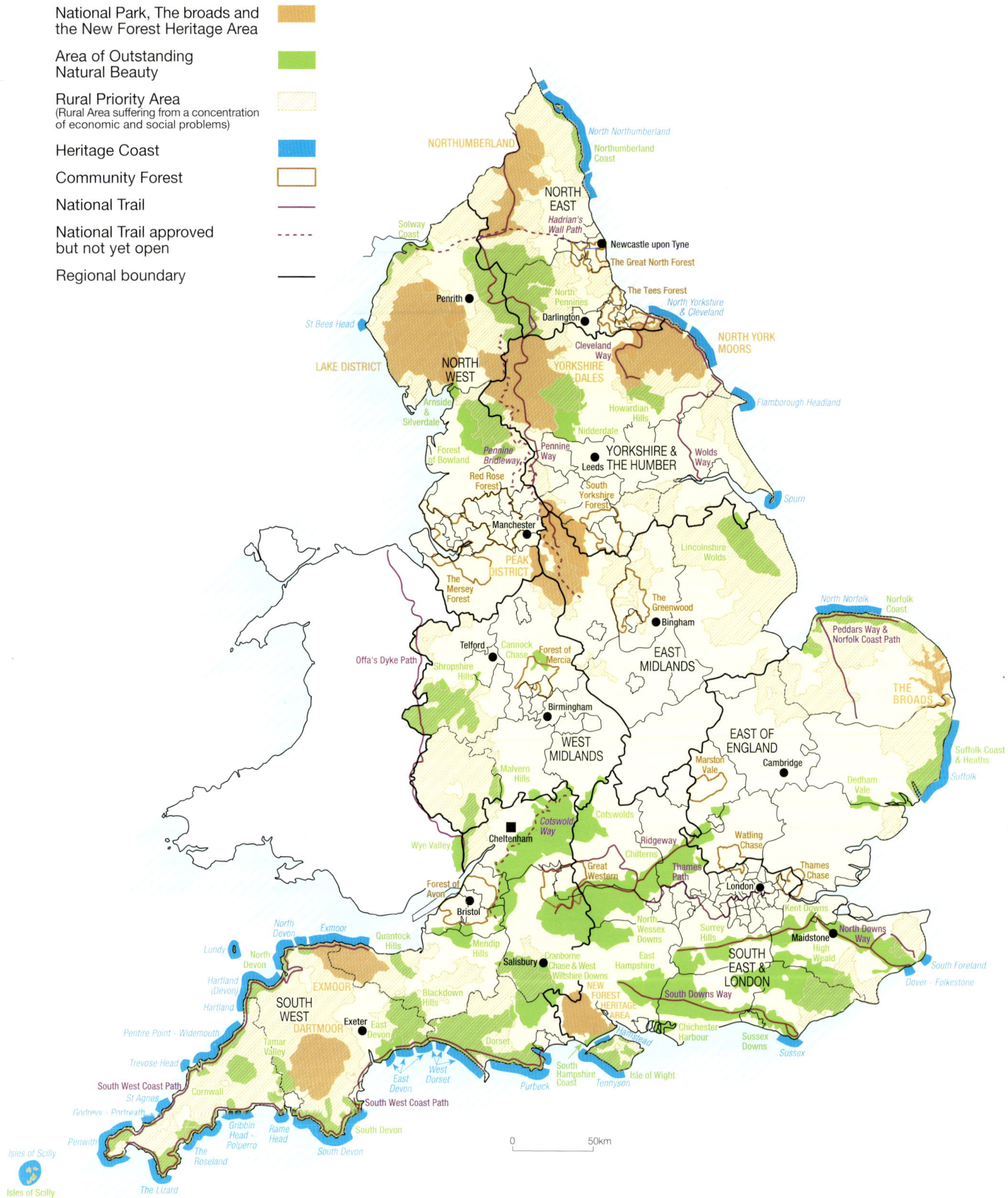

As at 1.4.2000